Her life for His friends

Her life for His friends:

A BIOGRAPHY OF TERRY McHUGH, 1950-1977

Cecelia D. Johnson

Fides/Claretian

ISBN 0-8190-0640-8

Cover design: Glenn Heinlein

Cover photo: *Philadelphia Daily News*

LC 80-25996

First printing, December 1980

Fides/Claretian

221 West Madison Street • Chicago, Illinois 60606

DEDICATED TO MY HUSBAND, BILL,
AND OUR CHILDREN, PETER, FRANCIS,
RICHARD, AND JOANNE

Contents

Introduction

The judge, who was an honest man, was seated on the bench of the federal court in Harrisburg, Pennsylvania. I was there as a character witness for one of the defendants. I was somewhat anxious. I did not know her as a member of the student body of Temple University, where I taught, but as a friend of friends, all of whom were full-time peace activists. The date was early 1971.

"Did the defendant enjoy a good name among her peers and the faculty members at Temple University?" the judge asked.

"Yes, sir,"

Little as I knew her, I was sure that much was true.

"Yet, she is accused of taking part in this action against the government, trespassing on federal property with the intent of destroying official government records. And you tell me you think she enjoyed the respect of her peers at Temple University?"

At first I thought he was indulging in a heavy irony of a sort that eluded me. Then it dawned that he really meant what he said. I was in Squaresville, U.S.A., the venue chosen in an attempt to gain a conviction of the Berrigan brothers on a charge of conspiracy to kidnap the Secretary of State. I think it had not occurred to me until that moment that there were responsible adults so out of touch with student sentiment during the Vietnam war that they could harbor opinions like the judge's. She was our Joan of Arc in residence. The silence lengthened. I had to answer.

I knew enough not to read him a lecture about the state of the nation, especially about its youth. I cannot remember exactly what I said—probably something not on the judge's wavelength but calculated to do no harm to the cause of Terry McHugh.

I did not see Terry much after that. She escaped indictment by a grand jury and, in general, got off lightly. The testimony of her former priest-moderator in the Catholic Youth Organization had stood her in better stead than mine, I am sure. Happily, the question of what the Community Service Corps van was doing outside the federal building on Cherry Street never came up. But the priest made the best possible case for Terry. We all would have. We thought we knew someone rather special.

What was proven by the brief career of Theresa McHugh, I think, is that Catholic elementary and secondary education sometimes "works." There are always people sitting there in front of the much-maligned sisters and layfolk, the brothers and priest teachers who take the whole thing seriously. They think that evangelical justice has to be taken at face value and that when the popes cry out for peace, they mean it. What they do about it often terrifies their teachers and sometimes fills them with awe.

I cannot say I have. met a Catholic school graduate thoroughly inoculated by the gospel who was not prepared for it by a stiff dose of ethical uprightness at home by at least one parent. There may be such graduates. I have not encountered them. I do know many who have become deeply interested in the venture of faith when neither parent cared much about belief, but there was some religious practice.

Having met numerous members of the clan McHugh in

the courthouse that day, I nonetheless knew nothing of Theresa's family background. I only knew a teenager who spent most of her time after the high-school day seeing to the needs of the poor. Later, a faculty member of my university's School of Social Administration could not praise her highly enough. She fulfilled all the hopes that the faculty had placed in a two-year associate program, forming paraprofessionals.

What went into Terry McHugh? What formed her? I'm sure I don't know. I can only say that she created an ineradicable impression on me in the few times that I met her.

And now a generous friend, who knew her much better than I, has asked me to supply this word of introduction. I am delighted to do so. Although not very perceptive spiritually, I think I know when grace has crossed my path. It did in the person of this young woman. I should like many others, readers, to have the same experience.

GERARD S. SLOYAN
Professor of Religion
Temple University,
Philadelphia, Pa.

Prologue

"My backpack is nearly ready. It's on the floor by the door at home. I checked the list and still need some items: two bandannas, one pair of running shoes, one pair of heavy shoes. Somebody said to get Vietnam jungle boots. Can't you see us trekking through the pines in Vietnam jungle boots? It's downright laughable.

"After we get to Maine, they take us to the island by boat. They told us, 'You'll be warm, happy, cold, wet, tired, and hungry.' I have always wanted to go."

Outward Bound survival camping is for the fittest. Hurricane Island is a rugged, three-week stint. Human ingenuity overcomes nature. To be subdued by it would be devastating, not to mention extremely painful. Three days of it will be solo in some desolate part of the island. Three matches are all you get to light a fire. Not much food either. Some fruit and chocolate; for the rest you're on your own. Each person has a whistle and can blow for help if things get really desperate.

A group from Discovery Leadership Institute was invited to Outward Bound. The DLI is part of the Community Service Corps of the Archdiocese of Philadelphia. Terry will supervise five teenage boys. Scholarships from the camping school made it possible for them to go. They leave in a week.

"Outward Bound. That's when a ship casts off and heads for the open sea," Terry continued. "It sounded so great at the briefing. I got goose bumps when we heard that we will 'leave our moorings.'"

Friday, July 1, 1977 was a typical muggy day in Philadelphia. Wet air hangs heavy over the rivers through much of the summer. Maine should be cooler. Even the jaunt to the Jersey shore, to say goodbye to her folks, offered Terry a breather.

"When I come back from the shore, I'll pick up my gear and meet the kids. Then we'll board the train for Boston, find our bus for Maine, and come back in twenty-five days, to be exact."

The shore traffic was bumper-to-bumper crossing the Walt Whitman Bridge into Jersey. As it thinned out on the expressway, Terry lit a cigarette and settled behind the wheel of the van. The van. The old van was worn out and the tires were thin, she knew, but at least it was paid for. Except for an occasional sputter and a sluggish pick-up the ride to Brigantine was smooth. Terry needed the break after rushing through the day.

"Forty miles to go yet. I can smell the salt air already. Aunt Liz used to say she smelled salt air as soon as she got on White Horse Pike." Terry mused. "I've had so many good times at the shore. There was that day at Margate when Joe Corley borrowed a bus. We took sixty little kids from north Philly to the beach. Bobby Todd went with us. Sixty children. They burst out of the bus when we got there. Scattered. It was like they couldn't get enough freedom. They had never seen sand before or the endless ocean. Joe yelled at me. Man, was he mad! 'Why did you let them run off? Terry, how could you do that?' I felt awful. We got them all together though. I hated making Joe mad. I must have felt awful for twenty minutes.

"Then there was the time I was at Avalon with the Search crowd. That was a real kick. There we were, on the beach playing 'touch.' I caught the ball, and Rev-Nev chased me into the water. All the time, I was waving to the FBI guys who were parked on the street, close enough to keep their eye on me. Poor guys, they were working.

"Well, that's all gone now. Forgiven but not forgotten. We'll have fun tonight. Friday night at the shore. The whole family will probably be at the Circle Bar. Sort of a send-off for my trip to Maine. Any excuse for a party. We're one family that loves parties."

Joni Mitchell came on the radio singing "The Circle Game." Terry sang along:

> Yesterday a child came out to wander,
> Caught a dragonfly inside a jar,
> Fearful when the sky was full of thunder,
> And tearful at the falling of a star.

The song reminded Terry of a little girl's birthday party. Terry loved the children, wrote about them, and had given the piece to a friend to critique.

Kelly was three when she said, "Terry, I'm too little." And our eyes met. She climbed all the way to the top and I was behind her. Together, we saw a world from the top of a playground sliding board. Together, we decided we weren't ready. And I was twenty-four.

Kelly's fifth birthday was only two days ago. She sat on the porch by herself. She sat at her tiny table with her tea set. Her eyes looked confused. Her lips quivered and her freckles were touched with delicate tears. I kissed her hand.

I watched the children at the birthday party. Marnie was putting pennies in the piggy bank. Jennifer was coloring. Megan stood in the corner, shyly. And then someone said,

"Come on, it's time for birthday cake." The children were hesitant. "Come on, we're going to have ice cream and cake now." Marnie put the pennies down. Megan came. Somebody got Kelly. And so the children came. "What's wrong with these kids, they don't like ice cream and cake?" And they laughed.

Later, it was time to play "Pin-the-tail-on-the-donkey." It was scheduled. And the children said they didn't want to play. They stood them in line and taught them how to play anyway.

Then later, Kelly's mother said, "Kelly, did you thank Megan for her gift and for coming to your party?" I remember how Kelly's little body tensed as she threw her crayon to the floor and shouted, "I said thank you. I said thank you. I said thank you!" She left the room to sit at her table on the porch. She was alone, and I kissed her hand.

Now, I'm scared again, and I am twenty-six. Fear of something which is cloaked in false, empty language. And so, I write a story to tell of truth. And now, I am ready.

Terry's story ended here, leaving unexplained what it was she was ready for—and leaving it to another to tell her own story as well and fully as possible.

1. A Time of Change

There is a lingering fear in giving up the old vision which has provided pre-dictability and consistency.
John Powell, S.J.
Fully Human, Fully Alive

Clusters of people, murmuring, watching, gathered across the street from 2202 Heather Road. Bike riders glanced toward the house as they coasted back and forth. A stone flew through the air and hit a window. Another cracked it.

The house was the second in a long row of brick rowhouses in a new section of Folcroft, in Delaware County, Pennsylvania, a quiet, blue-collar community. Horace and Sara Baker had dared to buy a house. They moved on the Saturday of Labor Day weekend, 1963, and when their car sat overnight in front of the house, neighbors knew that the Bakers actually expected to live in the terraced, hedged community.

The next day paint splattered the car. Insults and threats came from the ever-present cordon of neighbors. The Bakers took asylum inside their house, venturing out only to the store, conscious of their conspicuous, unwanted blackness.

Not all Heather Road people threatened the Bakers. Some were noncommital, and a few said hello to Horace on

his way to the market. Surprisingly, a handful of welcome
cards came in the mail. Even so, the attitude of the majority surfaced in contrived harassment and wore Horace
Baker to the breaking point.

Every summer for 30 years before, a rash of localized
interracial housing incidents flared in northern cities.
Catholic Interracial Councils formed across the country to
mediate conflict and promote understanding. Working effectively in New York and Chicago, the councils were often
an antidote to festering fear and bigotry.

The Philadelphia black population was contained within
well-defined boundaries. In the '40s, the ghetto spilled
over into changing neighborhoods, and young blacks and
Hispanics mixed with aging whites. The Second World
War brought a "second emancipation." Inner-city houses
bulged with people who had run from unemployment in
the South to find work in the North. As the war effort
wound down, black unemployment surged, and poverty
became a major scar on the profile of Philadelphia. The
church's attitude was one of service and benevolence toward blacks.

Crossing denominational lines was rare and awkward,
regardless of race. Catholic wounds from 19th century
hurts were remembered and rehashed by grandparents.
Catholics stalwartly defended doctrines of the church. The
Catholic Evidence Guild stood firm in Vernon Square in
Germantown, explicating dogma. Catholic youth flung
themselves into Catholic Action. Orphans picnicked in
June; gazed at Christmas displays downtown in December.
Fraternal organizations filled tables of the poor with
Christmas baskets.

The poverty culture was seen as a natural condition.

Usually, black children felt themselves outside the system before starting school. Still, no one disturbed apartheid. By rigid custom a popular movie theater in northeast Philadelphia relegated blacks to the back rows. Without question, only blacks used the 4th Street beach at Ocean City, a New Jersey shore resort. And, in Kansas City, theaters kept the last row in the balcony open for blacks. If the show was bad, two rows were open.

Rumblings of a black revolution seared the status quo. In 1955, Freedom Riders in Montgomery, Alabama moved from the back seats to the front on buses. Rosa Parks, a 43-year-old seamstress, would not budge when the bus driver demanded that she give her seat to a white man. Rosa was already in the back of the bus, and she was expected to stand when the section for whites was overcrowded. She refused, was arrested and fined $10. Blacks, led by Martin Luther King, Jr., boycotted the Montgomery bus company. Mrs. Parks' refusal opened the way for King to lead the growing civil rights movement. In November, 1956 a U.S. Supreme Court decision ended segregated bus service, and the boycott ended. People sang about it:

> If you miss me in the back
> of the bus,
> you can't find me
> nowhere.
> Come on up to the front of the
> bus, I'll be ridin' up there.

For the most part, however, the '50s plodded along with the constants: homespun values passed from one generation to the next, so did lifestyles; a child's future held few options; money and social class defined the boundaries of mobility. America was solid.

Children of the '50s were entranced by the Mouseketeers and Princess Summerfallwinterspring. Values were formed by a moving image that skillfully aimed to convince and convert. The TV generation was on its way to becoming the NOW generation.

A farmer's son from Bergamo, Italy realized the fulfillment of his priesthood when he became bishop of Rome and pope in 1958. Angelo Guiseppe Roncalli, Pope John XXIII, through the Second Vatican Council, sparked life into a church bogged down with legalism and brought hope into a world rushing into the nuclear age.

The grandson of a Boston Irish immigrant was elected president of the United States in 1960. John F. Kennedy turned the hearts and hopes of America toward a "New Frontier." He inherited the problems of Vietnam which, so far, was merely an ankle-deep skirmish.

When the United States launched its space program in 1962 and when worldwide communications bounced off telestar satellite systems, all humanity broke with the past.

On August 30, 1963 just a few days before Horace and Sara Baker moved to Folcroft, 20,000 people marched in Washington, D.C. to protest civil rights abuses. They marched for jobs and freedom and to petition the Kennedy administration to pass civil rights legislation.

The country was in turmoil. A credibility gap widened between the facts and the official reports of events in Vietnam. The U.S. sent 5,000 more troops to fight a war not yet declared. The poor and uneducated were likely candidates for the draft. At home, on a different battleground, a cry of the innocent pitifully echoed through the states: At 10:22 on a Sunday morning, September 15, 1963 a bomb exploded in a black Baptist church in Birmingham, Alabama. Four girls had excused themselves at 10:15 to go to the washroom. As white plaster dust fell, rescue workers searched the pile of bricks where the washroom once stood. Deep in the rubble they found the remains of the girls. The 16th Street Baptist Church had been the center of civil rights rallies.

Pumpkins decorated the doors and windows of the houses on Heather Road early in October, hurrying Halloween. In the preceding weeks, news of resistance to blacks moving into the area spread through the media: more than a summer flare-up, it came across as a sign of the times, a symbol of change in America.

Catholics who had been working in interracial affairs since the '30s and a number of young black Catholics who had a less sentimental, more activist view, rallied together. The more vocal of the group met with the pastor of Folcroft's Catholic parish. He saw the conflict as a parochial problem and preferred local resources to deal with it. Disheartened, but not defeated, the group, about 30 in all, took to the sidewalks. They listed the names of people who had made some overture of friendship toward the Bakers. Pairing off, they visited each home, encouraging the neighbors to persevere. If all those who were accepting would come together, the neighborhood might deal with its problem effectively.

A tinge of autumn spiced the air when four people drove across the city to Folcroft on a Friday night. The safety and confidence they shared in the car cooled as they looked at the long row of anonymous white doors.

"O.K., we ring the bell. Then, what do we say when

somebody answers?" Joan asked. Joan had come from northeast Philadelphia, a sprawling area of row homes with a hundred potential "Folcrofts." The northeast's one percent black population had been neatly parcelled during the Civil War.

Dennis thought for a moment. "I think we'll just say, 'Hello, Mrs. Smith, we're Catholics and we have come to talk with you about the Bakers who have moved here recently.'"

Ringing doorbells went well. However the desired cohesion did not happen. The environment worsened. Frustrating confrontations between homeowners ensued. Horace and Sara Baker, the silent victims in the crisis, moved out.

The people working to improve the Folcroft situation drew together to revitalize the old Catholic mechanisms for dealing with black problems. To benevolence toward blacks was added the current push for equality, especially in the minds of young blacks. An interracial group emerged with a new name, new methods, and in a short time, 300 new members.

The Catholic Community Relations Council, CCRC, worked forcefully at creating better understanding within parish organizations; exchanged home visits between black and white families, all the while in communication with the diocese through its president, Robert M. (Mitch) Thomas.

Mitch, a public relations expert, was a young black convert who was, as he put it, not a cradle Catholic. He had been brought into the Folcroft situation by Dennis Clark and Anna McGarry who saw themselves as Christians doing Christ's work.

When Mitch Thomas spoke at a meeting of the Catholic

Youth Organization in Center City, he told what had been happening in dealing with race problems. A slender, Irish, reddish-blonde, sixteen-year-old sophomore plied him with questions. There was something gentle in her movements, something feminine. She weighed maybe 100 pounds. Her green school uniform made her look thinner. Mitch saw an unguarded openness in her smile.

"Where do you meet? Are high-school kids in your group?"

Mitch was encouraged. These refreshing young faces could bring a new spirit into the hopelessness of many inner-city black people. Then too, they might be a bridge of understanding in their own homes with their parents.

"We're developing plans with Father Finley in Most Precious Blood parish for what he calls pre-evangelical work. I think you'll fit in beautifully. . . . Your face is familiar," Mitch said, "What's your name?"

"Terry."

"Give me your address, Terry. We'll let you and the CYO know how our plans develop. . . . Hey! I've seen you at church, Our Lady of Lourdes."

"When McHughs all go together, we fill two pews," Terry grinned.

Her smile was a greeting, an embrace. She radiated an inner drive, and Mitch soon realized that other people caught the spirit that flowed through Terry McHugh.

After the Folcroft debacle had quieted, the chancellor of the diocese called a group of priests together. Monsignor, then Father, Philip Dowling, who was a theology teacher at St. Charles Seminary, drafted a paper on the teachings of the church on race and ecumenism. Vatican II was the guideline. His paper was the opening statement on the formation of the Cardinal's Commission on Human Relations in May, 1964.

"The very deep problem in Folcroft brought out the need for guidance to pastors in racial unrest," Monsignor Dowling says. "Then, Vatican II was going on at the same time. So, a single agency had a twofold purpose: ecumenism, a way to reach out to others, and interracial work, a way of coping with racial crisis. Both were equally important. There was no blueprint. Our first effort was consciousness raising."

About the same time, two priests became aware that high-school students were learning more about basketball than social justice. Fathers John Nevins and Francis X. Schmidt, who were teaching at Cardinal Dougherty High School in Olney, Philadelphia, introduced the idea of students going out to serve others.

Eventually, they met with Father William Finley who was then assistant pastor of Most Precious Blood, a parish in the heart of the Strawberry Mansion area.

Philadelphia is a conglomerate of small towns with names that go back, in some areas, to Revolutionary times. Strawberry Mansion is a section of north Philadelphia that has seen better days. Fairmount Park sprawls along its border. Music lovers can go to Robin Hood Dell on summer evenings and not see or be touched by the blight that festers in the narrow, noisy streets to the east.

The priests realized, on the one hand, the need to challenge the students in Catholic high schools. On the other, black youngers in elementary schools desperately needed help with reading and math. After school, many inner-city children went home to empty houses. It was lonely. When parents returned home from grueling work, they were often too tired or simply not capable of going through the rigors of their children's homework. Black children in public schools were losers before and after the last bell rang.

By September, high-school volunteers were tutoring in eight inner-city centers; six new basketball leagues formed. A year later, Community Service Corps became a big umbrella for expanding programs that, eventually, would touch nearly every facet of interpersonal need within its scope. "The students, and the people they meet, see what true religion and true charity really are," said Father Nevins. The CSC dovetailed with the Cardinal's Commission. Both welcomed mutual support.

The whole country, in fact, was awakened to the call of an outgoing spirit. "Take a sad song and make it better," the Beatles sang.

2. The Shoppe

*Nobody can minister to his fellow man
when he is unwilling to deny himself
in order to create the space where God
can do his work.*

Henri J.M. Nouwen
Creative Ministry

The din was deafening in the cafeteria of West Catholic High School for Girls. Terry heard Tootsie Browning say something to her about "after the last class." For a moment she dreaded the possibility of having to stay for one more rewrite of a composition she had bungled in English class.

Tootsie, who had abandoned her name, Adrienne, to record books and formal occasions leaned closer, spoke louder.

"Sister Carolyn wants to see you after school."

"Wow! That's a relief. Bueno, porqué, que pasa?" Terry looked soberly, directly at her friend.

Tootsie preferred to limit Spanish to Sister Carolyn's Spanish class. Nevertheless, she thoroughly enjoyed it when Terry tried to look serious.

"Oh, come on, McHugh. Porque. She didn't say *why*," Tootsie answered, "but I guess it's about CSC."

Sister Carolyn Cadomo, a petite, intense Sister of Notre Dame de Namur, moderated the Community Service

Corps at West. When she saw Terry at the end of the day, she told her she had a phone call from Bob James, president of the Catholic Community Relations Council.

"They have a store-front building near Most Precious Blood church. It's a thrift shop and has lots of space where we might be able to help the children who go to the public school. Bob said they really need more help than they get in school. Will you go in there with me to meet him?"

"Sure," Terry said without hesitation.

Then she wished there were more days in the week. Always on the move, she was in: CYO at her parish, Our Lady of Lourdes; Surge, an ecumenical youth group; CSC at school; CSC central; basketball; and softball. School work plagued her, especially any kind of writing. Somehow she felt this new challenge in the inner-city was right for her.

The stores on 29th Street had seen more prosperous times. Not long ago Strawberry Mansion was a clean, busy neighborhood. Now some people won't stop in the area, even during the day, for fear of being mugged. Many residents hesitate to walk the street because of gang fights. Iron grating has protected the doors and windows of stores for years. In the late '60s, the building at 2205 was empty. A three-story store-front, it stood dark and dilapidated, a reminder of life once lived there. The graffiti sprayed on walls was typical. Initials and aimless scrawls were drawn by "artists" who left before the paint dried.

In the light of day, for all to see, one fledgling was intent on filling an empty spot with his name. Either he ran out of paint or he could not spell, because when a blurred TIR appeared, he hesitated.

"Tyrone, stop that!" someone yelled.

Tyrone threw the paint can to the curb and darted up the street.

Members of the Catholic Community Relations Council wanted to rent 2205. They wanted to take the church to where the people were and to where the children were because, sure enough, the people were not coming to the church. They would sell good, donated clothes, cheaply, in the store. It could also be a center for neighborhood children to fill the emptiness in their lives.

One look at the place and a practical person would have said, "Forget it." It needed plumbing, a new heater, paint from first to third floor, and the fire department wanted to close it up because there was no way out if the front door was blocked. A tiring search for the owner was fruitless. The building was condemned; the resale value, zero. Bob James, Bill Johnson, vice-president of the Community Relations Council, and Father Finley enlisted the help of Cursillistas to fix the plumbing, find the paint, and fire up a new heater. The CCRC claimed the place. The Shoppe opened in the fall of 1967.

On a Sunday afternoon in February, 1968 Sister Carolyn and Terry met there with Bob James. Bob, an energetic 33-year-old black, had vision and insight. He had recently been appointed to the Cardinal's Commission on Human Relations and was concerned, specifically, for the welfare of his community.

They agreed: the youngsters in the area needed to know that they were loved and accepted. After talking a while, Terry went upstairs. She saw the clutter. Looking in room after room, she realized the tremendous job ahead; the renovation that was needed to receive the children. She saw the possibilities, too, for warmth and hope that could soon flow. Going outside, Terry met some children who were curious about the signs of life in the old store. Her smile disarmed their suspicions. They giggled and gibbered. Terry was touched by the children's awkwardness in expressing themselves. There was a definite need for a program in speech and reading skills.

"Since the children were so lovable and seemed so receptive, I decided to do what I could to help the situation," Terry said.

Every Saturday into early summer Terry came with friends from CSC, and seminarians from St. Charles, the diocesan seminary. A faded maroon T-shirt, jeans, work shoes and a green army cap easily and persistently identified Terry. The crew heaved rubble out windows, scrubbed floors, and painted walls. They scrounged for rugs and old school desks. A rope ladder dangled from a rear window with the approval of the fire department.

Tootsie Browning's fondest memory of renovating The Shoppe will always be the removal of the cast iron, four-footed bath tub. Too heavy to budge, the tub had to be broken into parts. Bobby Todd appeared with a sledge hammer. His virile whacks demolished the last vestige of a former era. Quartered and useless, it was poised on the pavement.

Children who lived nearby soon caught on to what was happening at 2205 and became co-workers in the metamorphosis.

Time was the factor with Terry. Traveling on buses took hours. Her parents sighed with relief when she arrived home safely. Terry had a driver's license a few days after her sixteenth birthday, although she learned to drive long before her permit was issued. Quite often she saved time driving from her home in Overbrook to 29th and Susquehanna, using the family car. In the summer of 1968, she drove her father to work first and saw the early morning sun cast long shadows across city streets. Terry caught the excitement of each new day. Other volunteers came to The Shoppe about 8:30 a.m. and were not surprised to find Terry in the kitchen, already making sandwiches for the thirty or so children who would need lunch later.

A summer program called Discovery Prep was launched by CSC. Activities were enhanced by Terry's talent for discerning the needs of others. Children who had no conception of a world beyond the streets surrounding their red-brick rowhouses viewed the panorama of the Philadelphia skyline while splashing under the fountain at Logan Circle. On the way to a picnic at a Bucks County farm, fifteen children, including Terry's sister Maggie, packed into a station wagon. Terry drove. Tootsie Browning and Beth McMullen shared the driver's seat. Out of the city and onto suburban streets that had no sidewalks, the car whisked down a hill on Easton Road. Terry nudged Tootsie and in a whisper said:

"Don't yell, don't scream. We have no brakes."

All the while gaining speed, Terry spotted a gas station, where the road began to incline. Now in a lower gear, slowing down, the car headed for a pile of tires and stopped safely in a mound of rubber.

There were less adventurous trips to museums. Then too, the children took pride in the art work they did in The Shoppe. When the day's events ended after lunch, Terry stayed in the neighborhood to visit. Sipping tea in their parlors, lonely old women were refreshed by Terry's laughter. Seeing the children in the streets around their homes gave Terry insight into their many volatile episodes at The Shoppe. She felt at home in the black ghetto.

A white person, especially a young woman, walking on side streets, provoked hostility in some blacks. One angry young man spat on her. She was aware of the danger. At a luncheonette, on a rainy August afternoon, three black teenage boys sat at the counter near Terry.

"What you doin' here, Whitey?" one demanded.

She turned toward them, leaned her arm on the counter and said, "I'm doing what you *should* be doing."

Terry was certain that her gifts had to be given in that specific part of the city. However, within herself the force of conviction clashed with fear. Doubt walked side-by-side with Terry. A spurt of faith never failed to outdistance doubt.

"From there on," she said, "I just kept running into situations where I saw oppression. I realized you have to respond to a situation where you can. Where there's lack of concern for human life, then you have to do something about it, no matter how small."

In September, a team of high-school students came to tutor at The Shoppe, led by Terry who was starting her senior year. They were eager to meet fifth and sixth graders from the McIntyre School. In they came every day after school, tutors and children.

There were no crucifixes on the walls, no holy cards or pictures of saints—just people. The people brought the church and its message to 29th Street. Unadorned, unencumbered, and penetrating ... people-to-people, person-to-person. Terry at the hub. The children came for help with homework, reading and math. They came for cookies and milk and for the warm feeling of being wanted.

It is hard to say why Tyrone came, although a first guess might be that he was a junior Weatherman bent on destruction. A calmer, second guess is closer to the fact: at age eleven he read on a first-grade level. He heard that he might get help at The Shoppe. Ashamed and angry because he could not keep up in school or read baseball cards or comic books, he was overwhelmed. No one had shown him the stars from his dark pit of hopelessness.

On a Friday afternoon, when a tutor was about to give up on Tyrone because he was noisy and unbearable, Terry said she would stay with him a little longer. She sat in a desk beside him and read a paragraph, word by word. She emphathized with him. He echoed her words, slowly. She asked him to take the book home and practice the words each night over the weekend. Ready to argue, Tyrone frowned.

"You gonna pay me?" he asked, sullenly.

"Pay you!" Terry said, "no, but I'll pray for you."

He groaned but took the book with him.

On Monday the children and volunteers came to The Shoppe again. As they hustled up the stairs to the second floor, Terry heard them giggling and humming songs they would soon be singing. Tyrone walked with the others, not shoving, not inciting to riot. He went directly to Terry and read the paragraph.

"Talking with one another is loving one another," he read slowly. "It is the light of the Lord that shines in all bodies." Suddenly he looked up.

"Did you pray for me?" he asked.

Terry said gently, "Yes, I promised to pray for you, Tyrone, and I did."

"I love you." Tyrone smiled shyly and was silent.

Terry hugged him.

When a minister realizes that he or she can give life to people by enabling them to face their life-condition in friendship, anger dissolves. Energy that was spent on fear converts toward empowering the positive purpose for which each person is created. Latent potential develops. The givers will, at the same time, cease looking at themselves as persons in a limited, introverted reality. An expanded vision of life results and real joy of spirit.

Bill Johnson, who lived in all-white northeast Philadelphia, believed the CSC students' exposure to the black milieu would, in turn, improve their parents' understanding of the black experience. Bob James says it was a fantastic summer. He envisioned The Shoppe as a family center. He saw it as a vital part of the universal movement toward harmony with all people. Terry wanted to expand the program to include preschool children who could come while their parents worked.

The Shoppe thrived for almost three years.

3. When Did You See Me Hungry?

Youth ministry involves first and foremost not programs but relationships.

A Vision of Youth Ministry
U.S. Catholic Conference

It was a warm day in the spring of 1968 when Bob Todd first met Terry. He was younger than Terry, a sophomore at Eustace High School in Camden, New Jersey, having transferred from Dougherty. His loyalties stayed with the Philadelphia CSC. They stood outside the CYO building on Arch Street, celebrating the end of a long, gray winter, enjoying the sun.

"She was thin as could be, looked like a mouse," Bobby remembers well. Her hair was golden in the sunlight and bangs fell flat across her forehead. When Joe Corley, a young seminarian joined them, they went indoors, all reluctant to leave the balmy air. Father Schmidt told them about the plans for the trip to "Resurrection City."

The Poor People's March in Washington, D.C. to an encampment around the Lincoln Memorial during May and June developed an aura of subdued protest and mounting grief. Martin Luther King, Jr., the instigator of the march, had been assassinated only a few weeks earlier on April 4, 1968. The very presence of nearly 100,000 people made a statement to Congress to pass legislation that would bring justice to blacks.

June 19 was Solidarity Day. Twelve delegates from Philadephia's CSC joined the march that day, passing out pamphlets, acting as couriers and absorbing an invaluable learning experience. Although Joe Corley was aware of a tense atmosphere, Terry was completely at ease. "She was bubbly, fun to be with," Joe says. "She even managed to get through the crowd and meet the folk group, Peter, Paul, and Mary."

On the way home, Bob and Joe talked with Terry about the needs of the people who lived around The Shoppe. An understanding of the plight of the disadvantaged had seared them. Joe made The Shoppe his summer apostolate. Bob decided to go there every day. More than a little resentment gnawed at his parents, however. They had left the restlessness of Philadelphia to seek a better family life twenty miles away in a small New Jersey town. It was convenient to make Todd's house the first stop on the way home from Washington. Mrs. Todd had food ready. In fact, she had it ready the day before, not knowing that the CSC had made reservations for an overnight stay in the capital.

When Bob came into the house a day late by his mother's schedule, the greeting was icy, then turbulent. Terry went to Mrs. Todd and spoke to her gently. The storm subsided. After the goodbyes and thanks, Mrs. Todd turned to Bob and said, "It's a good thing you had that little one with you!"

Not only could Bob not break his ties in Philadelphia, he cherished the new ones The Shoppe provided. "I wasn't into any big cause," he says, "I loved being with those kids in the inner city. I just loved the kids."

The song lyric, "the times, they are a'changing," aptly described the state of flux of the late '60s.

The sign of the kingdom as a remote, ethereal existence embodied in long black habits of nuns changed to an empathic meeting with humanity when some sisters donned street clothes. Sister Carolyn's order was one of the first to change and choose to identify with the served. Leaving the enclosure of the convent, three sisters of Notre Dame de Namur moved into an apartment on Susquehanna Avenue, near The Shoppe. The owner of the building, a two-story rowhouse, loaned it to Father Finley for parish use. He, in turn, made the second floor apartment available to the sisters. During the school year Sisters Pat McNeil and Sarah Fahey did graduate work at Temple University, not far away. Carolyn commuted to teach at West Catholic High School. However, Carolyn's proximity to The Shoppe made her a bona fide neighbor and gave more credibility to her desire to communicate with area residents. During the summer, she was the respected keeper of the wrench that opened the fire hydrant on a street secluded from traffic. Gushing water cooled hot little black bodies; Terry at the center, exuberant.

Three mornings a week the program at The Shoppe included a swim at a nearby city recreation center. Moylan pool was reserved from 10 to 11 a.m. Invariably, a group of hefty toughs cluttered the entrance. Not exactly a greeting committee, their stares and barbs made Joe Corley cringe. He feared that his height, short hair, and white skin branded him as a condescending do-gooder. "They saw us as invading their territory," Joe said. Although it never happened, he often feared seeing the glistening steel of a switchblade pointed at his ribs. Each step inside the gate was an assertion of faith. Terry appeared nonchalant but was equally aware of the awesome possibilities. Safely in, safely out: they trusted in the Lord.

Those busy days were timeless. Actually, the economy of the neighborhood slightly improved. Terry, versatile and untiring, taught the girls to sew. She showed them how to cut patterns for dresses that flattered the shapeless figures of ten-year-old girls. Terry used her many talents. Adept with a hammer and saw, she was just as nimble with her sewing kit. Evidently she learned by watching her father shape the patterns her mother used in making clothes for their nine children.

On Friday evenings The Shoppe took on a different character. For one thing, business boomed in the store. Volunteers from CCRC worked behind the counter selling clothes at prices proportionate to a person's income. A man's suit went for $2.00; a lady's blouse, 25 cents. The council believed that respect for paying customers did more for their dignity than being on the dole. They became consumers in a consumer society. The oppressive burden of powerlessness eased a little.

Then about eight o'clock a gang called the 29 D's sauntered in. The area of 29th and Diamond Streets was their turf. They sat around a table upstairs and rapped with a few CCRC members about their lives, their problems and goals.

Occasionally at dusk the frazzled young CSC staff gathered together around a priest. In the quiet of a back room, away from the wail of sirens, they began the great prayer of thanksgiving and hope. They walked every day with the mystery of suffering. Terry, especially, bore the anguish of ambiguities. Her constant conflict was to reconcile the truth of her inner convictions with the obliviousness of the majority of society to the despair of the poor. Very few shared the intensity of what she saw as right. She was impatient with people who did not see the Christian imperative in scripture, Matthew 25:31–46:

> When the Son of Man comes in his glory, escorted by all the angels of heaven, he will sit upon his royal throne, and all the nations will be assembled before him. Then he will separate them into two groups, as a shepherd separates sheep from goats. The sheep he will place on his right hand, the goats on his left. The king will say to those on his right: "Come. You have my Father's blessing! Inherit the kingdom prepared for you from the creation of the world. For I was hungry and you gave me food. I was thirsty and you gave me drink. I was a stranger and you welcomed me, naked and you clothed me. I was ill and you comforted me, in prison and you came to visit me." Then the just will ask him: "Lord, when did we see you hungry and feed you or see you thirsty and give you drink? When did we welcome you away from home or clothe you in your nakedness? When did we visit you when you were ill or in prison?" The king will answer them: "I assure you, as often as you did it for one of my least brothers, you did it for me."
>
> Then he will say to those on his left: "Out of my sight, you condemned, into that everlasting fire prepared for the devil and his angels! I was hungry and you gave me no food, I was thirsty and you gave me no drink. I was away from home and you gave me no welcome, naked and you gave me no clothing. I was ill and in prison and you did not come to comfort me." Then they in turn will ask: "Lord, when did we see you hungry or thirsty or away from home or naked, or ill or in prison and not attend to your needs?" He will answer them: "I assure

you, as often as you neglected to do it to one of these least ones, you neglected to do it to me." These will go off to eternal punishment and the just to eternal life.

She struggled with doubts: the force of her inner direction spawned the question, "Why me?" As in St. Luke's Emmaus community, Jesus affirmed his presence in the breaking of the bread. The Eucharist renewed their spirit.

Most of the white students who went to The Shoppe met resistance from their parents. Tootsie Browning could go only when she was accompanied by a friend. Parents feared for their children's safety. Worse yet, the CSC work in the Strawberry Mansion area was a mute subject in many suburban homes. Parents not only did not want to hear about it, but some students found it necessary to leave for The Shoppe without saying where they were going. Others merely dropped out.

The children who were accustomed to seeing Father Finley on the street mistook his name and called him Father Friendly. When he was transferred from Most Precious Blood Church to another parish, the pre-evangelical aura of openness that had developed in the neighborhood was not nurtured by the new pastor. Even so, programs at The Shoppe expanded. In the coming year they would be bolstered with funds from the Philadelphia Anti-poverty Action Committee, the federal Office of Economic Opportunity, and the archdiocese. All together, nearly 500 CSC volunteers worked with 11,800 inner-city deprived youths in schools and churches in 1968. But, The Shoppe had its own unique style.

Terry was elected vice-president of CSC central. She and Al Puntel, the president, shared responsibility for using organizing skills to keep the programs running smoothly. Bob Todd, the itinerant from New Jersey, used his ingenuity as program developer. Terry, however, had the rare ability to develop leaders and the willingness to free them to lead.

By August, Terry had to start thinking of her coming senior year. An early warning signal came on the postcard giving her the date and place to be fitted for green oxfords, uniform footwear for West students. Thoughts of school stirred mixed emotions in Terry. She had to deal with the regret of quitting varsity basketball because Sister Carolyn had suggested giving more time to The Shoppe. She was eager to be a senior; she was already 18 and by legal standards, no longer a minor. The prom and graduation were things to look forward to eagerly. In a fleeting fantasy, she imagined herself at the prom in a plaid shirt, jeans, and work shoes—the last prank.

The hype of senior activity was tempered by her sluggish academic pace. Terry knew she was intelligent. Her insights were like a laser beam. She was beginning to agonize over the escalating Vietnam war. In her social consciousness she saw the tangled implications of inner-city decay. Yet, simultaneously, she had to labor over studies in the lowest track of the school. Reading had been a problem from first grade on. A poor start spiraled into stress over school work, although she always managed to maintain her grade level. Some teachers commiserated with Terry's quirk; others lost patience and accused her of being inattentive, dumb. While some people would anesthetize themselves from the pain of such a personal contradiction, Terry confronted it with aggressive perseverance. Over and over, she scrutinized her writing, correcting "saw" for "was," "no" for "on." After taking notes in class she checked with a friend to catch mistakes.

Frustration caused sadness which she carried alone. To her world she gave an effervescent smile. It was a beckoning to come forth.

4. Hanging in There

With this compassion you can say. . . . In the depths of my being, I have met my fellow man for whom nothing is strange, neither love nor hate, nor life, nor death.
Henri J. M. Nouwen
With Open Hands

At a notably bland convention in Miami, August 1968, Richard Nixon was nominated the Republican candidate for president. His party had taken extreme precautions against eruptions of young war protestors. Later in the same month the environment of the Democratic national convention in Chicago was the most violent in U.S. history. Even though Lyndon Johnson had rejected any idea of renomination, antiwar protestors were on hand to shout their disapproval of his leadership in the Southeast Asia war. Hubert Humphrey was nominated as the Democratic presidential candidate, but the convention paled in the presence of 10,000 militants' angry protests. Pot-smoking, draft-card-burning demonstrators camped out in Grant and Lincoln Parks. "A Festival of Life" they called it.

Chicago police, state police, and national guardsmen routed the protestors and drove them out of the city parks. The festival became an ugly foray. The upsurge of anti-establishment feelings of the '60s erupted in that crisis.

The role of leadership was being questioned in the late '60s. It was not just a lack of confidence in particular leaders; it was the evolution of attitudes toward leadership itself and toward the sharing of responsibility. The tragic assassinations of President Kennedy, Martin Luther King, Jr., and Robert Kennedy shook the country's reliance on the lasting, steadfast role of leaders. Then too, maturing people realized that their voice must be heard. In the political sphere, a few firebrand activists submitted to the discipline of the democratic process and ran for public office.

The church welcomed Pope John XXIII's practice of collegiality. The terms "people of God" and "Christian community" identified a new perspective, and the siege mentality that had insulated former generations dissipated. In many Catholic groups the mind of Christ in special apostolates was discerned through communal sharing. Some leaders, instead of demanding blind obedience, facilitated the potential of others. The value of inner discipline became more important than external conformity. Ideally, a bureaucracy could neither denigrate nor interrupt the wholeness of each person and each community in Christ.

The Second Vatican Council provided timely wisdom. The Decree on the Laity launched a broadside against the confusion of the day. Pointing out that human lives have become increasingly autonomous, it seemed to anticipate uncertainties. "Conditions demand that their apostolate be broadened and intensified."

The young-adult generation was swept along in the spate of changing times. An unusually abrupt transference from one era to another was beyond their understanding or control. Again, the compassionate words of the Decree on the Laity spoke directly to them: "Young persons exert very substantial influence on modern society. There has been a complete change in the circumstances of their lives, their mental attitudes, and their relationships with their own families. Frequently they move too quickly into new social and economic conditions. . . . They seem to be unable to cope adequately with the new burdens imposed on them." Calling young persons "apostles of youth," the council asked them to reckon "with the social environment in which they live."

Bob James was full of hope. He and his wife Harriet saw the coming of a new day when their children could live in one society. As young black parents, the prospect of remaining reclusive distressed them. Bob had quickly agreed with the Kerner report from the National Advisory Commission on Civil Disorders that said white society condoned the black ghetto it had created. Getting to the heart of the matter, Bob was aware of two Catholic churches: split by color, the church was a reflection of society. His bitterness mellowed as he saw new life being pumped into his parish. Full of admiration for Terry and her CSC helpers, Bob said, "We know that a generation will come along that will turn this nation around. A generation will rise up and not see color, but will have a goal to live out the belief in the right we all struggle so hard to prove."

By the time of year when the old heater warmed the radiators of The Shoppe, Terry was beginning to see good effects in the children. They were much more open to her, to their tutors, and to each other. They were learning what it meant to relate to other people.

"I found that influencing children at an early age helps break down barriers of race and even authority," she remarked.

Terry had no delusions. She did not see herself as a leader although she eased into the role. Her "big, open heart," as one friend put it, her intelligence and ability to organize placed her in the forefront. Terry preferred to give others the confidence to lead in things she initiated. Probably the proof of her leadership quality is the fact that she could move on and not be covetous of projects and her role in them. Friendship was most important to Terry. Persons came first, programs second.

Sharing the leadership of the general CSC with Al Puntel was no burden for Terry. However irksome to Al, Terry was off helping other people much of the time. One meeting of high priority with other CSC officers was delayed in starting, waiting for Terry who never showed up. She forgot. Nevertheless, she checked into the central office almost every day. Marge and Charles (Bud) McHugh had resigned themselves to their daughter's shuttling from one activity to another. For peace of mind, they insisted that all of their children call before boarding a bus to come home. When Terry told them she wanted to go to Jamison, Bucks County with the CSC for a Search weekend, their parental concern sharpened. They had never heard of Camp Neumann and knew nothing about its supervision. To them, Search was one more label on one more program.

After Father Nevins heard of Cursillo, he wanted the teenagers to have the same experience. Father Schmidt learned that a parallel format for youth, Search, was successful on the west coast. The two priests introduced it in Philadelphia just in time for young people who were seeking maturity. The world had grown up overnight and left them with basic problems and questions. For one, who am I?

Terry threw herself into the Search weekend with her usual abandon. She shared the energy of life that electrified the 50 high-school boys and girls who were with her. It was a dynamic experience in Christian living. Those 48 hours spent apart from everything somehow brought everything together. That one segment of time gathered the fragments of her life and made it whole. Although her family was imbued with the meaning of Jesus' message, the church, the protector and overseer of the message, seemed remote. Religion had become impersonal and regimented. When mission clubs at school raised money through competition between classrooms, the drive to be best was stronger than the desire to minister to people who were not being fed in body or spirit. Terry saw much effort go into collecting money for people far away. She held no resentment, but bore some pain in her awareness of the mission closeby. The missions far away were a priority at school, while many children of the poor in the very same city had to go to school without breakfast. She herself knew that Darlene Moore, a black girl near 29th Street, suffered from malnutrition. Terry had become acquainted with the gospel early. Her youthfulness was mature in faith and in the word. She clearly understood its meaning and was conscious of a minus sign between the medium and the message. Search seemed to bring them together.

Search made it possible to personally experience Christ at the center of life, in the smallest happening. Search was a new beginning. Not like a retreat, the weekend was free-flowing, sometimes raucous, always enjoyable; a time to find a new attitude and deepen faith. For most who go, even the team, it is a peak experience. Re-entry can be a problem. Sometimes euphoria dims in the patchy fog of an uncomprehending world.

While Search is a journey you make only once, Terry soon became part of the team, spending many weekends at Camp Neumann. There, the Mass embraced her in a communal love stronger than death.

Terry quickly developed rapport with the central CSC staff who also led Search weekends. Early in November, a few CSC people sat in a basement office at Arch Street and brainstormed ideas for a Christmas activity. Father Schmidt had been given boxes of toys. He also had names of families who were badly in need of help. "See what you can do with them," he told Bob Todd, "maybe you can come up with something." "That was a great thing about "Schmitty," Bob says. "He'd just hand you an idea, a really adult kind of job and say 'see what you can do with it.'"

"So, who has any ideas about how to give out the toys?" Bob asked.

"It's dumb to just go up to a house and hand a kid a toy," Pat said. "Could we sing carols or something?"

"Yeah, it looks like we're doing them a big favor on *our* Christmas," Bob added. "We really should make the families feel like they are part of the celebration, really make it mean something."

"You know, it should work both ways, too," Terry said, "It'll give our kids a chance to meet people who have a really tough time getting along."

Before long, Bob ordered costumes: ten Santa Claus, twenty elf and twenty clown outfits. Nearly one hundred CSC volunteers went on Christmas Eve on "Operation Santa Claus."

Terry, dressed as an elf, Joe Corley, as a clown, went with Bob Todd who was Santa. It took hours longer than they expected. House after house, people invited them in. "Have a drink," the father insisted. Grapefruit juice and gin was one house specialty. Down the street, rum and coke.

Between visits, Bob turned to the others and, through his full white Santa beard said, "I'm used to guzzling a few beers, but I can't handle this!"

"But we'll insult them if we refuse," Joe said.

Putting the back of her hand to her forehead, Terry said, "I feel like I'm getting the virus. Hey, if we keep this up I'll be Rudolf the Rednosed Reindeer for sure."

They went on to the next address singing Jingle Bells and lavishing abundant cheer.

Operation Santa Claus became a major yearly activity of CSC. Forthwith, however, Father Schmidt issued a directive: No alcoholic beverages are to be consumed while distributing toys in the program.

A few days after Christmas, Bob Todd called Terry. "I have to talk to you about something. Can you meet me in town?"

As they ambled down Chestnut Street, passing store windows that still glittered with decorations, Bob stopped for a moment and looked at Terry, "I really felt down Christmas Eve after the thing was all over—that whole Operation Santa Claus bit. It took so long to get it all together, and it was a hell of a lot of fun. You know, I felt like I was part of Delgado's family, like I could have stayed there longer, and at some other houses, too. Then, when we got back to Arch Street and went into the chapel. . . ."

Terry listened. Terry had the gift of being present without distraction. She gave unreserved attention to whoever needed her. It was easy for her to listen to Bob. "Wow, he's cute," she thought to herself and held his hand.

"You expected to still be in a party mood but instead you felt let down? Maybe it was the drinks," Terry said.

"Ter, it wasn't that," Bob said, not smiling. "When I got up front in the chapel and turned around, I saw everybody laughing and clowning. I felt they missed the whole point. They were getting more out of it than they put into it."

"Bobby, you put more into it than most of those kids. And, after the rotten stuff we see in the summer, I guess you come at it from a different angle." Terry tried to calm him.

"Right, they talk the talk, we walk the walk!"

"Yeah, I know how you feel," Terry looked down at the sidewalk. "Like, it wouldn't help Darlene Moore much to give her a Barbie Doll when she needs good food every day."

"I've had it, Ter, I'm just disappointed. I don't think I can work on it again," he said, "I guess I've been reading too much lately about paternalism and all that stuff."

They had walked slowly and had reached Independence Hall.

"It's hard when you see things other people don't see," Terry said.

"There was this priest in Jersey," Bob went on, chopping his words. "Some people knew he was in touch with families on welfare, so they gave him money for twenty turkeys. A donation from their organization. Twenty turkeys. You know what he said?"

"Go stuff 'em?" Terry asked, ready to laugh.

"Well, he might as well have told them that. He thanked them for their kindness. Then he said he would give them twenty names and addresses and they could take the turkeys to the people themselves. And he told them to think about asking each family if some of them could come and eat the turkey with them. They didn't take the addresses, and they didn't give him the money either."

"Ain't that a kick," she said.

Terry had an innate sense of what could be done to give hope to those who are trapped in need. She also knew, as did Bob, that well-intentioned gestures cause hopelessness to surface. Givers who are enjoying the good life in a free society enhance their own status, and the receivers feel more powerless. In Terry's view, tokenism was the ultimate insult. Palliatives looked good but she thought true Christian charity ought to try to find out why help was needed, get the facts, and work to change things.

An inner voice gave her answers but also caused her to live with a great deal of doubt. Her silent struggle was to reconcile the truth of her own convictions with the persistence of empty tradition. She realized that she needed the institution to succeed in meeting the needs of impoverished people. But, at the same time, her own response to the reality of those people called for innovation, departure from custom, and direct action. Therefore, it was necessary to reflect in solitude on every critical situation. With scripture as her reference she followed the lead of her inner direction.

At that time in her life it was important to persevere with friendships. She did not want to merely use the CSC; she treasured the relationships. She could put up with differences in perspectives in order to save an interpersonal relationship.

"I've got to believe," Terry said, "that a lot of the kids who went around with us on Christmas Eve will be touched by the people they met when they have a chance to think about it. Bobby, I'm going to try to hang in."

"O.K., Ter, you hang in."

5. Here's To Life

Empty and dark shall I raise my lan-
tern, and the guardian of the night
shall fill it with oil and he shall light it
also.

Kahlil Gibran
The Prophet

Terry's five sisters and three brothers unmistakably re-
semble their father. Terry, the third in the family, inherited the typical McHugh nose, short and slightly rounded
at the tip; keen, attentive blue eyes; sensitive mouth, always ready to laugh; and a chin that juts out just enough
to offset the curving slant of high cheek bones. Her voice
was throaty. Terry grew taller in her senior year. Her hair
touched her shoulders. Parted on the side, the bangs dis-
appeared and most of the time a sweep of stringy blonde
hair was tucked behind her ear. She wore glasses, on occasion, that deceptively made her look intense. By choice,
her wardrobe was not frilly or lavish. In winter, she wore a
hooded car-coat with toggles. The tan collar of her uniform blouse was always starched stiff as a board, so stiff
that it frayed her uniform. Tootsie Browning envied Terry's stiff collars and tried to get the same effect.

Mini-skirts were the "in" fad. While outside the school
building, the girls had a way of shortening their skirts by
tucking them in at the waist. Hems were hiked. Inside,

hems dropped, leaving just a bit of knee exposed. Knee socks covered the rest. Terry did not go along with the fad, although once or twice she was asked by a watchful nun to kneel on the floor in the corridor. When her hem touched the floor, she had met the required length.

Terry trudged through school work, hoping to graduate. Experiences with the children at The Shoppe gave her the desire for more skills in child care. She wanted to enroll in the Child Development program at Temple University. But first she had to graduate. Typing class was her nemesis. When she went to the CSC central offices to practice typing, she slouched over the typewriter to hunt and peck at a snail's pace. It never got her down. Far from fretting over it, she would laugh. Her main interests were elsewhere. Mainly, the winter tutoring program at The Shoppe took much of her time.

Terry's never-ending hours on buses were cut considerably when the Cardinal's Commission bought a van. It was blue and had white lettering on each side:

COMMUNITY SERVICE CORPS
CARDINAL'S COMMISSION ON HUMAN RELATIONS
ARCHDIOCESE OF PHILADELPHIA

The van was entrusted to Terry more than anyone else. The CSC needed transportation. It was a boon for Shoppe activities. Looking for even more convenience, the closeness of Sister Carolyn's apartment to her work in the neighborhood made sense. The sisters agreed to have Terry live there in the summer.

The three nuns were becoming more and more concerned about the Vietnam war. They met regularly with the Catholic Peace Fellowship, a local group of about 30 activists. The speed of Terry's typing was a low priority compared to her growing interest in the peace movement. Although she was influenced by Sister Carolyn, Terry formed her own arguments against the war. At school, Masses for peace reinforced her convictions which came from her scripture-prayer-centered spirituality.

Even though the school acknowledged the seriousness of the war by offering liturgies for peace, students and faculty were not to be identified with the school in outside peace actions. On a Monday morning, after being in a weekend peace demonstration, Sister Carolyn was advised, as a teacher, that she was getting too involved. The students were told not to wear their uniforms if they went to peace rallies.

Shortly after his inauguration, President Nixon said that he would end the war in the next two years. Contradictions chipped away at trust in his promises. On April 24, 1969, U.S. B52's dropped 3000 tons of bombs on the Cambodian border near Saigon. It was the most intense bombing of the Vietnam war. Later, in June, Nixon announced the withdrawal of 25,000 troops. Still, 525,000 remained and more than 30,000 had been killed. U.S. military tactics changed with the use of defoliants and napalm. Airborne chemical sprays stripped miles of trees bare and made it difficult for enemy troops to hide. Vegetation was ruined for years to come. Jellied gasoline (napalm) spewed from low-flying aircraft and firebombed straw villages. Vietnamese people ran from under the fiery cloud. Whether war was being waged or winding down, it was controlled by the Nixon administration.

It was the pictures of naked, burned children that rent Terry's heart. The injustice, the indefensible injustice. A friend in the Catholic Peace Fellowship understood Terry's feelings. "Anyone who can emphathize with the poor, to be with and experience what the poor experience, can also feel the plight of war victims—know what it's like to be speechless."

Terry's parents, whose patriotism rode high throughout World War II, did not question our involvement in Vietnam. Though saddened by it, the war seemed necessary to meet the communist threat and contain the Russian bear. Expressing her views at home caused conflict, so Terry kept them to herself. It was quite natural for her to not disclose her thoughts to others. She was not secretive, not two-faced; she simply believed that her thoughts and activities should not be flint for sparks in loving relationships. Neither did she try to convert anyone to her way of thinking. On the other hand, she could get testy when talking with friends about the war. Terry's personality had a large share of meekness with a reserve of a firecracker ready to blow. Once in a while, she would enter a situation with a few spicy phrases that got right to the point. As someone said, bluntly, "She could get mouthy." However, when it happened, it was after long agitation and not a surface irritation.

With it all, Terry had an irrepressible sense of humor. It was fun to be with her at The Shoppe. On a humid summer afternoon in '68 she heard rumbles coming from the third floor. Running to see what was wrong, she found that everyone was throwing papier mâché. Wet globs of pulp flew through the rooms. In a moment, she was into it, throwing and dodging. It ended with Derek Green standing four feet tall, totally molded in papier mâché. At other times the laughs were of the Keystone Cops variety. More than once, when Joe Corley drove Tootsie Browning and Terry into Center City, he slowed down at Logan Circle. The girls jumped out of the moving car, ran through knee-deep water, under the fountain, fully dressed, sans shoes and hopped into the car as it came around.

During the school year, some seminarians from St. Charles traveled by bus to inner-city apostolates—a sort of practicum. The group that headed for Most Precious Blood school took the E bus which carried a high percentage of black passengers. Dressed in black suits, black fedoras, and carrying black guitar cases, they were conscious of people staring at them. One passenger asked, with a tone of hostility, "What are you, gangsters?" They said they were not. "What do you have in those cases then?" "Guitars." "Prove it!" While riding along, one of the seminarians took his guitar out of the case and began playing. In a short time, people were singing "This Little Light of Mine," and a couple danced in the aisle. Negro spirituals were favorites. On many bus rides to the apostolate, thereafter, the seminarians provided music.

All through the country, changes in modes of dressing were visible expressions of the world's state of flux. Boys' and girls' hair styles were identical—shoulder length. Boys' hair, if not shoulder length, was longer than the neatly trimmed crew cuts of the fifties. Afros became popular. Sons' beards, too, shocked staid parents. Pants suits, leisure suits, jeans, and T-shirts pervaded the American scene.

It became important to be immersed in happenings. People needed people, and emotions were no longer stifled. The insistent beat of rock music had an experiential quality. While it was not meant to be much more than entertaining, rock and folk music of the day had the inherent effect of forming value judgments in young listeners. Protest songs and freedom ballads were effective in planting their message. The plaintive voice of Joan Baez called for peace. Television moved into the house much the same as a welcome companion for restless children and lonely old people. It served as an entertainer and educator. Beneath the threshold of consciousness, the tube inveigled viewers to want its products. A Jesuit priest, Neil Hurley, tried to prepare people in 1965: "By way of television and satellites, the moving image is becoming the universal language, the global educator. Perception of life has been retrained without awareness and without implicit consent." Television influenced Terry's life in a way that most likely fostered her outgoing disposition. "The mass media have helped our generation to become more concerned for mankind than ever before," she said. "In our own living rooms, through television, we can see what's happening throughout the whole world. Young people today respond in an active way."

The '60s was a decade of change. In his book, *Future Shock,* Alvin Toffler said that people were becoming dispirited. They will be programmed right out of their personalities. Trapped, the fundamental needs of the inner spirit will be unfulfilled. Technology was effecting spirituality. The key word in the last quarter of the 20th century was *flexibility.*

When Vatican II ended, its decrees were not enforcable laws. Rather, the essence of the council was the call for a change of heart, a metanoia. Some Catholics "went along with the changes" half-heartedly. Others welcomed them. While basic tenets remained intact, perspectives shifted from fear to love of God. Love of neighbor was renewed in equal importance. The dogmatic rigidity of religion classes eased into a less formidable presentation of the humanness of Christ. Tension pervaded parishes, classrooms, and religious orders. The council wanted the people of God to "renew the temporal order: take the spirit of the gospel out to others." The missions were not only in the South Pacific. Instead, mission is wherever a person walks.

Some reacted: Keep the church and the world separate; women should wear hats in church, it's the law; the poor are poor because they're lazy; don't ask questions, you'll be told what to do.

Others responded: The church is in the world, pray and get involved; don't make a fetish of the law; when we see the poor, we're poor too, and we're all the richer for it; I've got to be me, let's talk.

Fortunately, Terry had a good grasp on the idea of a changing church. She helped younger students who were confused by having to leave the well-defined Baltimore Catechism. Marie Forish, then a sophomore, says that Terry was a balance for her in school. Terry was a witness to how spiritual values affect everyday living. "Those values were her first priority. But she didn't preach them," Marie says, "except in talks on Search weekends. She lived them. I wanted to know what made her tick."

Terry applied for entrance to the religious order, Sisters of Notre Dame de Namur and was accepted. After much thought, she decided not to go. She feared being bound by rules and regulations. She was inclined to deepen her spirituality but was pricked by the fear of losing freedom of spontaneity. Chronic questions in Terry's mind were whether or not her strong self-direction could exist in a life of submission to another authority. Would the heads of institutions look approvingly on her need to follow her charisms?

When preparations for the summer activities at The Shoppe got underway, Terry told her parents that she wanted to live with the sisters in their apartment on Susquehanna Avenue. The McHughs were concerned about someone her age living away from home in an inner-city neighborhood but reluctantly agreed when Father Schmidt assured them that her presence there would be an asset.

Terry packed a few clothes, some record albums, and her favorite pillow and went to stay in the apartment.

Susquehanna Avenue was narrow and busy, one of the few two-way streets in north Philadelphia. The apartment was a short distance from The Shoppe and a little farther from Most Precious Blood church. In a crowded neighborhood, rowhouse dwellers assume a separateness, a hidden detachment once inside their houses. Carolyn and Terry lived in the area specifically to try to overcome the separateness and encourage the openness of community.

The apartment was small, although the living room was ample. A rear window overlooked a litter-strewn lot. There was barely enough room in the kitchen to turn around after a table and chairs filled a corner. The sisters ate sparingly because of a meager budget. Spaghetti and sauce was the staple diet. On Terry's first night, Carolyn added meat balls and an inexpensive bottle of wine. "Gracias a la vida," she said as she raised her glass. Terry hesitated, thoughtfully, and smiled, "Right on—here's to life."

Philadelphia sizzles in the summer. Acrid air lays pocketed between the Delaware and Schuylkill rivers. When clear dry Canadian air revives the city the days are gems. Shadows are sharp and cool. In the suburbs, the smell of new mown grass sweetens the air and at night trees are black and still. Even the noise of traffic is hushed. Noxious fumes evaporate, and grateful Philadelphians savor the relief. North Philly has pitifully few trees. An oasis of grass grows on the side of Most Precious Blood church. A park in a square here and there offers breathing space in the center of long rows of houses with white marble steps. People sit on their steps at night in the summer. A portable radio propped on the shoulder of a passerby blares then fades. Other people shout conversations at each other from opposite ends of a block. The ever-present whine of wheels rounding a corner and the screech of tires deny ghetto residents respite from noise. On hot nights the apartment was oppressive. Too often, a rock group practiced in a back room of a house at right angles to the building.

Soon after she moved Terry prepared The Shoppe for summer activities. Discovery Prep got under way. Neighborhood children between nine and thirteen years of age came for fun and help. Going on at the same time in Most Precious Blood school, and five other sites in the city, Operation Discovery offered teenagers courses in art, music, writing, and speech. The students were accepted on the basis of merit. Operation Discovery was beginning its sixth summer. Another program, Operation Outbound took the seven to twelve age group on trips to Valley Forge and other parks. All of the programs were supported by funding and staffed by full-time volunteers turned professional, being paid a salary. Terry shared hers with a friend who needed money desperately.

Carolyn and Terry concentrated on Discovery Prep.

"The best thing we had going there," Carolyn said, "was the rapport at a young age between black persons and white persons." Their hope was to motivate the children to be concerned about the inner city when they became adults. Terry believed it was especially urgent to develop leadership in the older children. She was resentful of large sums of money going to pay for Operation Outbound buses. Not that she wanted to deprive the children of a chance to see other places, but she thought there should be fewer bus trips and more neighborhood development.

The mainstay of support for The Shoppe came from the Catholic Community Relations Council. Although their treasury was dwindling, they had faith in their purpose. There was a growing breach with the parish rectory. The pastor, in fact, suggested that The Shoppe close. He preferred to have all activities involving Catholics confined to the church compound. After heated discussions, members of CCRC continued to run The Shoppe with his tacit approval. It was a strain, however, and the hope for this apostolate began to fade. Its days were numbered. Perhaps because he was not part of the inception of the idea, the pastor could not see the value of that kind of ministry.

Nevertheless, the children came each day. Living among them, Terry was more attentive. She was the high point of their summer. They teased her about her freckles. Some of the teenage black boys said they liked her hair, then asked if they could touch it.

Terry was delighted when Joe Corley returned to work at The Shoppe. He was three years older, a few inches taller. She thought he had been given a generous share of good looks. Joe related well with children until his patience ran out. Then Terry stepped in to restore his composure.

She would have tried to talk him out of staying in the seminary if she had wanted to serve herself. When she asked him crisply, "Why do you want to stay in the seminary?" he knew she was thinking of his good and not her own. He knew that she wondered if he would be able to serve people in the same way and "not be in jail," as she put it.

Terry was ready to get each day started. Early in the morning she used the van to pick up Joe and a few others. They sang folk songs on the way to The Shoppe. If Joe had to sum up what it was like working that summer, he would simply say, "It was a lot of fun." Terry was rarely depressed. She seemed to ride the crest of a wave and her spirit affected others.

An incident that put her in a somber mood happened at a picnic. Even though it was cloudy, they walked to a park closeby. The children played on the swings until it began to drizzle. Then they all gathered together under a tree and sang while someone played a guitar. A few yards away and across the street, they saw a rat crawl into a cellar window. The people who lived in the house were sitting on the steps and watched it. Terry was disgusted. It was not only the sight of the thing that got her down, she knew that people in that block had been asking the city for weeks to send Rat Control and no one had come. The people had no clout, no voice. They did not count. Terry shared their emptiness and suffered because of it. Joe thought he knew black people while he was in the seminary, but during the summer he realized his associations had been stilted. Until then, he had not coped with confrontation on the street. Living in the area, Terry knew how to deal with challenges. Joe felt less secure. They stepped out of the door of The Shoppe one afternoon when the children had gone home. A black man who probably had been drinking all day, staggered up the street. When the man slurred, "Hey, Whitey," Joe felt uneasy. He was ready to run when the drunk demanded to know what they were doing on *his* street. Terry walked toward the man and said, "Hey, want a cup of coffee?" He said, "No, honey," and continued to talk with her, simmering down.

Whenever Terry had the van it was usually packed with little children. Twenty crammed in for a trip to the zoo. Fifteen another day, when they went to an art exhibit at the Civic Center. When Terry and Joe drove in the van alone they talked about the Vietnam war. Joe had no definite stance about it except that he did not question the U.S. involvement. Surely, the government was justified. Terry had convictions that she expressed as if they were backed by knowledge. She seemed to draw from a well of information in forming her opinions.

In exasperation Joe asked, "Ter, where do you get all your evidence?"

"I just know it isn't right," she said, "it goes against what I believe in. We have no right to be there."

"Oh, come off it," Joe said.

"I've talked with some of the guys around Susquee who are back from there. They tell me a lot of stuff goes on that nobody gets to hear about in the news. We've got troops in Cambodia and Laos. Did you know that?"

"No, but I don't buy what you're saying," Joe said.

"I'm serious about it, Joe, and I go to the Catholic Peace Fellowship meetings to learn more," Terry told him.

"Some people are always looking for a cause. Terry, I hope you know what you're doing," Joe chided.

"It's not just a 'cause' for me," Terry said, "I *believe* in what I'm doing."

"What's the difference—a cause or a belief?" Joe asked.

"Well, a cause is something you march for and get all emotional about—sort of an ideal that's outside of you. I think when you really believe in something, it's part of you and you go along believing no matter what."

Joe gradually became aware of Terry's naive intuition regarding what was happening in Vietnam. Yet, he remained guarded and did not allow her to think he was impressed with her stance. He began to think she had the gift of discernment. Later, he was convinced of it. "She had an intuitive sense of right and wrong. About 99 percent of the time she was right."

Joe knew that Terry wanted to measure up to the gospel. The important thing for her was to try. Terry believed that we are accountable for what happens to the world and, so, we must be involved in some way. She could not live with herself when she refused. If she had stayed away from Moylan pool, it would have been considered wise, prudent. The commonsensical, human side of the conflict within her said it was all right not to go. The inner drive told her that it had to be done. She went ahead in spite of fear. She was kind to the drunk because her oneness with Christ's spirit prompted her response to the situation. Her stance against the war was rooted in faith in scripture and a fierce love of humanity.

There is a grace the comes with taking the gospel seriously.

6. Breaking the Barrier

*Youth ministry involves the struggle to
present to youth a prophetic witness to
Christian life against the predominant
value orientation of the general culture, a struggle that renders supportive community all the more important.*
A Vision of Youth Ministry
U.S. Catholic Conference

Grassy slopes of Fairmount Park edge the Schuylkill
river as it flows through the city. Clumps of trees hang
heavy over the west bank. In the spring, cherry blossoms
speckle the east bank with hues of pink and white. Joggers
run a steady pace in all seasons. Near the Art Museum,
Boathouse Row is a Philadelphia landmark. For years row-
ing clubs have owned houses that are still reminiscent of a
time when the world moved at a slower pace. Their docks
slant downward for the easy lowering of sculls into the
murky water. College and high-school crews row upstream
and back, practicing for weekly races.

Fairmont Park was only a ten minute drive from The
Shoppe, and Terry and her friends would sometimes take
a break to go canoeing on the river. As they returned from
one outing, a torrential rain drenched the city. Next day,
Bob James went to check for possible damage at The
Shoppe and found a new crisis to be solved. A flooded

basement had left a ruined furnace. The Community Relations Council funds were too low to pay for a new one. While public funding paid for tutorial programs, the building itself was a CCRC project. Council members knew the prognosis and much like facing a dying relative, they grieved heroically: without heat there will be no winter activities. What's more, the row was doomed for demolition.

Not wanting to see an end to her work which was a leaven in the neighborhood, Terry hoped the whole venture could relocate across the street. A larger building would accommodate a preschool day-care center. The child-care course at Temple University would qualify her to run it. Bob James saw a family center already developing and wanted to enlarge it. Bill Johnson needed more time to make the people politically aware of their potential. They were used and abused by the city, landlords, and government. They needed to learn how to use the services they were entitled to as citizens and taxpayers. They needed to recognize abuse and raise a collective voice for justice. Not only would Father Finley have understood these goals, he would have encouraged them. His absence made a difference.

Equally important, the CCRC members intended The Shoppe to be a model and fully expected other active lay people to open similar centers in deprived areas of the city. In a remote way, their hope was confirmed when a woman came from Dallas, Texas. She was visiting a relative and heard about The Shoppe. Carefully scrutinizing all that went on, she planned to take the idea back to Dallas.

After five years of interracial involvement the council had opted for a person-to-person ministry through The

Shoppe. They proclaimed the gospel: "If a brother or sister is ill-clad and in lack of daily food, and one of you says to them, 'Go in peace, be warmed and filled,' without giving them the things needed for the body, what does it profit? So faith by itself, if it has no works, is dead." (James 2:14-17) It was at the expense, however, of not concentrating on developing a well-heeled organization. Neither had they made it an adult community action that could be autonomous.

Within the same span of time the Cardinal's Commission on Human Relations became the center for interracial and ecumenical work. The Community Relations Council and its work at The Shoppe was a small frog in a big pool. With its broad outreach, the commission drew volunteers from all over the diocese to its own programs. The council, on the other hand, regarded The Shoppe as "the market place" of the gospels. But it got lost in the vastness of the institution. The commission had to serve great numbers of people. Ecumenical services awakened congregations to Christ's call for unity, "that all may be one." (John 17) Educational series used the group process to try to knit neighborhoods and parishes together. Eventually, distribution centers supplied food for destitute people.

Nevertheless, summer at The Shoppe continued as usual. As Terry drove through the streets, she saw a certain beauty in the rowhouses. The utterly flat fronts met the sidewalk at sharp right angles and the flatness was relieved by four steps to each front door. Now and then, flower boxes spruced parlor windows. Some houses added a narrow sort of porch with a wrought-iron railing. On the corner across from the apartment, a porch-patio had a plastic awning and several hanging plants.

For every house that had a modicum of decency, ten were mere shells or, at least, in disrepair. The awful ugliness of poverty assaulted Terry's sensitive spirit. Houses stood windowless like gaping, toothless mouths. Some steps had crumbled. Corner stores—Smitty's cafeteria and Wild's variety—went out of business and iron grating covered cruddy windows. Empty bottles and beer cans littered entry ways; ever present dirt lay along curbs. Night and day loud canned music from corner bars pierced the air while little children played on the sidewalks.

The environment of poverty is a no-win circle. When a family wants to buy a house, it is impossible to get a mortgage if other houses on the block are boarded up. When the search for owners of vacant houses is unsuccessful, as with The Shoppe, deterioration is expected to spiral and therefore lending institutions will not take a risk. When a family living in a house owns it and wants to borrow money for improvements, the loan is denied for a similar reason—in a risky area, no one is trusted. Redlining is the term for the boundary of borrowing.

Over 50 years ago the narrow streets of north Philadelphia were prim and proper. The lives of white residents revolved around the family, the mill, and church. Unethical realtors took advantage of the rush of black people into the city. They offered fast cash to a few white home owners on a block and resold the houses to blacks at a sizable profit. One-family dwellings were then jammed with two and three black families. The remaining white residents panicked in fear of change and fled. Anna McGarry will be remembered as the gutsy widow who stayed on north 18th Street. She saw both blacks and whites being duped and became an advocate for justice.

Actually, the changes in neighborhoods spread like a brush fire. White people wanted to salvage property values, and the influx of blacks was an encroachment on white cultural values. To complicate things, white people expected blacks to assimilate a white value system while segregating them, confining them within boundaries by unwritten edicts.

Carrying it further, if blacks can afford to move to better houses in a white neighborhood they can expect resistance. They are not really free to choose; they are powerless.

As people are made powerless, violence, not control, is fostered. Violence breeds in powerlessness.

Perhaps the greatest division of all is in the bond between human beings. When communications break down, the bond dies. The breakdown of communications is a spiritual tragedy. Talking together, one-to-one or in groups, expresses a reality which is greater than words. When there is no communication transcending the walls people build, there is no bond. Charity is reduced to tokenism.

In the midst of poverty, the bond of love between diverse people is enriching; in the despair of powerlessness, it is empowering. Terry knew that. This insight was her gift which she shared with joy. She was a real role model for the theology of service, a witness of an authentically Christian way. Someone who knew her said she proved "there is a God involved with the poverty situation."

Terry knew the dignity of many inner-city people, their genuine courtesy, compassion, and humor. She also interiorized their pathos. "You can work and work and work," she said, "but you'll never really solve the problems with band-aid therapy. The basic problem is to change the laws, change the funding and where it goes. Knowing what I know now, I don't know why black people don't revolt."

Over 30 children came to The Shoppe each day. While most of them were regulars, new faces came and went. Terry and Carolyn acquainted them with the assets of their city—Fairmount Park, the Art Museum, and their own Smith playground. Many inner-city children know only their "square"—a term endemic to Philadelphia. The seminarians worked steadily. Bobby Todd, too, commuted from New Jersey for the second summer.

Bobby and Terry still had much in common. He was the CSC representative at the '69 White House Conference on Youth. Knowing how Terry's values lined up with all other value systems of the time, he thought she was one of the healthiest people he knew. She was full of life.

Bobby invited her to go to the CSC Inaugural Ball. Her year was up as vice-president, and new officers were elected. They accepted their new roles at a formal supper dance in a Center City hotel. Bobby was vague about the exact location of Terry's house in Overbrook. Fortunately a friend, George, was with him. As they drove down Wynnewood Road, a row of large twin houses, George said, "You'll know her house when you see a motor on a porch, a car motor."

"A motor!" Bobby said.

"Yes, she's working on one with her brother. She keeps it there so people can tell which house is hers."

Terry's style was uniquely her own. At 19 she was the youngest in the apartment on Susquehanna Avenue. Sister Pat seemed to feel responsible for her and watched her with a critical eye. The four managed nicely, however. About once a week a priest-friend celebrated the liturgy in the living room.

The owner of the apartment building, Chuck Hall, lived on the first floor. He was a young white man, deeply involved in social justice issues. In fact, it was Chuck's openness that resulted in the sisters and Terry living there. After having offered the building for parish use, Chuck and his wife Doris decided to make it their home. They were as interested in ending the Vietnam war as their tenants. By the fall of 1969 all the residents of 3007 Susquehanna Avenue were in the peace movement. To be antiwar is one thing; to be in the peace movement is quite another. One is passive. The second means becoming an activist.

During the Vietnam war years there were varying degrees of activists. As an example, Garry Trudeau started his Doonesbury cartoon strip. In a much more intense degree, nine Catholic priests entered the Selective Services office in Catonsville, Maryland and dumped hundreds of draft classification records into trash baskets. They took them outside and burned them as a symbolic protest. The Catonsville Nine. Philip Berrigan went to jail for his part in it, and his brother, Daniel, eluded the FBI.

Draft evaders hightailed to Canada.

In the capital and across the country, millions observed Vietnam Moratorium Day on October 15, 1969 by holding prayer vigils and wearing black armbands. In Washington, D.C., Nixon ignored it and Vice President Agnew called the leaders "an effete corps of impudent snobs." Again in November a second Moratorium began with a "march against death." Candles lit up the night, 250,000 in Washington and 100,000 in San Francisco: the biggest march in U.S. history.

The country was at loggerheads. The protestors were equated with a student-youth rebellion of leftists. On the right, a counterwave arose. Nixon soon described his traditionalist supporters as "the silent majority." Their silence, nonetheless, did not quell a crisis of distrust in all authority that shook the underpinnings of society.

Antiwar protestors gained credibility when Senator William Fulbright, chairman of the Senate Foreign Relations Committee, charged that the U.S. was conducting an undeclared, undisclosed war in Laos without the knowledge or consent of Congress.

When Joe Corley heard about Fulbright's statement, he remembered what Terry had said. He began to understand what attracted her to the Catholic Peace Fellowship. Peace activists began to frequent Chuck Hall's apartment. If asked, some of them would have known the whereabouts of Daniel Berrigan who avoided the FBI for four months, taking shelter in twelve cities with thirty-seven families.

Terry's parents were not happy with her mingling in that milieu because of her age. "The people were too old for her," Marge McHugh said. Despite Terry's independence and strong need to "do her own thing," she had no desire to be alienated from her family. She loved them, and although they did not always understand her, they loved her. She had a special fondness for her sister Joanne, who was fifteen years younger. Two other sisters, Ronnie and Maggie, often helped at The Shoppe. The McHugh family is an enviable entity.

Terry was a student in a new two-year associate program

at Temple University. After a practicum in child-care centers she would receive an associate degree. Temple was not far from the apartment and it was convenient to go to classes during the week. Her parents stringently insisted that she come home on weekends. Terry complied.

7. Seek and You Shall Find

*With constructive, enthusiastic in-
volvement of people who care, these
young persons will bring the healing
touch of Christ and his word to youth
who are lonely, frightened, and waiting for someone who understands.*

A Vision of Youth Ministry
U.S. Catholic Conference

Fortunately for Terry, entrance into Temple University's Child-Care Program was easy. It is unlikely that she
would have done well in College Boards. The two-year
course does not require an entrance exam; a high-school
graduate need only apply for the three semesters of inten-
sive classroom work. The fourth semester is a paid intern-
ship in a children's service agency.

Terry kept up with academic work, but it was extremely
tedious for her. In spite of the grind, she brought a lot to
it, probably more than others in her class except Tootsie
Browning, whose experience at The Shoppe gave her the
incentive to become a paraprofessional. They matched
their previous basic training to theories learned in class.
They knew that no textbook or teacher could define the
love, fun, and compassion of The Shoppe, both given and
received. Studying sharpened their skills, however, and
the children they had yet to meet would benefit.

When winter set in, Terry continued tutoring but no longer at The Shoppe. Discovery Prep centered in poverty-area schools. She became the sole driver of the van, transporting children from one point to another. It was impractical to return it to Center City each day; therefore, she had full use of it. The paint had lost its sheen, and the motor was a shambles. It had often stopped dead, leaving young passengers stranded. Terry usually managed to get it started. Fuming, she sent a letter of complaint to General Motors. Her bobby pins clamped wires together under the motor; the radio was hooked together with pennies; and, a wad of bubble gum sealed a seam in the dash. The van was a familiar sight around Susquehanna Avenue.

For no particular reason, Terry stayed at the apartment less during the fall. The hype of involvement in the neighborhood slackened. Although she often went home to Overbrook at the end of the day, many weekends were spent at Camp Neumann. Her parents were more at ease with her working on Search teams than in the company of visitors at the apartment. People flowed in and out of 3007 Susquehanna, upstairs and down, coming from New York, Boston, and Baltimore. Terry let them use her quarters when she was not there. It became a meeting place for peace activists, and Terry was taken into their confidence when they discussed possible actions in the Philadelphia area. While her identity with the movement centered on the Catholic Peace Fellowship, she found a commonality with Chuck and Doris's friends who were in the East Coast Conspiracy to Save Lives. It was customary for Terry to freely loan and freely borrow among friends. It was not unusual for her to loan the van to whoever needed it to pick someone up or just go out to buy a six-pack. For convenience, the keys hung on a pegboard inside the front door when she was there. Still, Terry was sensitive to manipulation and would back off if she thought she was being used.

When she worked on Search teams, it was with the same resolve that characterized everything else she did. There were 20 to 30 Search weekends a year between 1969 and 1972. Terry became identified as Father Nevins' assistant. "At a time when young people weren't into religious things," John Nevins says, "500 kids who made Search applied to be team members."

Camp Neumann nestles in a wooded area of Bucks County farmland. A long, rutted driveway leaves Old York Road and civilization behind. About seven o'clock on Friday evening teenagers, mostly from Catholic high schools, come in car caravans. White pillars on a porch of a large house can be seen in the darkness as team members show boys and girls the way to their cabins. If they were expecting wall-to-wall carpeting and color TV, the contrast is a shock. Sixteen stripped iron bunk beds line plywood walls. That's about all there is. Showers and a lavatory are enclosed in a corner. Outside, a few rusty chairs on a porch seem to say "Don't sit too long." In the distance a horse whinnies.

Terry was in her element in the rustic setting of Neumann. Her usual attire, including jeans and boondockers, was natural for the camp. At times, Searchers took the train from Philadelphia to Hatboro, a few miles away, and Terry met them with the van. She could sense apprehension about the weekend. A mixture of feelings caused tension on Friday nights—for many of the students, it was a lark to be away from home, free of parents. On the other hand, they were anxious about stepping into an unknown 40 hours, giving up free time. Everyone gathered in Gino Hall, a square, roomy cabin with a stage. Some of the less believing persons asked out loud, "What the hell am I doing here?" "How do I get out?" Terry eased the confusion somewhat with her own litany, said in one breath:

> "Hang loose,
> Be cool,
> Easy does it,
> Ya Ha!"

You could expect her to follow it with, "Gimme ten" both palms extended.

It was a difficult time of transition for students who had spent ten or twelve years learning objective morality. Certainly they did not refer to their religious training in that way. Yet, they saw God as a stern law-giver outside of themselves, and their relationship to him was judged by how they kept the rules. Self-centered spirituality got no further than a guilt trip. The Search experience began with talks that helped people feel good about themselves. There was a tremendous need to restore self-esteem. Feeling worthless and unlovable has a devastating effect on a person's idea of self. A poor self-image formed in childhood has a tendency to persist into adulthood. So before the concept of God, a loving father, and Jesus, a brother, could be introduced, the seeds of destruction had to be weeded out and those of healthy self-love sown. As one team member said, "When everybody gets comfortable, you talk about the Lord." Christ was "snuck in" another said. Various team members gave talks on faith, commitment, and the meaning of being a Christian. The ministry of the word is the sharing with others of the gospel message, the good news of God's love.

The kids broke into groups to share their thoughts. As in the story of the road to Emmaus, catechesis is effectively carried out in small groups where there is good feeling when joining together to reflect on their lives and experiences in the light of Christian faith. Sessions broke for swimming in warm weather, sledding in winter.

Terry's advice, "hang loose," described the weekends. However, there were a few firm rules. No alcohol was allowed. Every so often, a group came well supplied. On one memorable Search, boys brought wine and ready-made Manhattans. Father Nevins confronted them with the choice of handing them over or leaving. A black boy who worked on the docks during the week gave him a hard time, saying it was the first time he "sipped with white boys." He gave it all to Father Nevins, and he said, "You don't need this stuff to get high up here."

By Saturday night the people knit together in an authentic sense of celebration. An agape, a paraliturgy, closed the day's schedule. The music exploded into a lot of joy, a lot of singing.

For many teenagers, the Sunday liturgy was the first experience of a close, spirit-filled community at prayer. Bob McCarty, who worked on teams with Terry, remembers one Mass in particular. He sat next to Terry. She snickered when someone burped and then started to laugh. Her face turned crimson. She left the chapel knowing that her laugh, which got out of hand, might not be funny.

The same people who were lukewarm about starting Search on Friday night hated to leave on Sunday.

When Dave McKenzie went through the Search weekend, it had no effect on the sadness that filled him. Dave was ill, always in pain. Rarely without a headache, he had hydrocephalus—water on the brain. He had prayed to get better but gave up, thinking God did not care about him. He still found hope in living and put energy into high-school activities. He ran for president of the student government. A teacher was surprised when Dave won and said, "Wow, we didn't think you'd live to get out of high school." The prospect of dying had not occurred to Dave. He was stunned. It was true; his illness was that serious.

"From then on, I lived with death," he said, "I gave up on life. Death ruled my life." Resentment toward God burned inside him. He wanted to know that he counted. Instead, he was empty and angry with God. Once, in a chapel, he lashed out: "You son-of-a-bitch, God! Why did you do this to me?"

John Nevins asked Dave to work on a Search team. When team leaders witnessed to healing during their talks, he began to listen. The bond of community is disarming. It enables a person to put hang-ups aside and hear others. And, in doing so, to hear God speak.

On his first weekend as the team leader, Dave's attitude turned completely around. When he heard his friends tell about their faith in the Lord, he believed. He was no longer negative about life. He knew God cared about him. From then on his health steadily improved. As he went through college, he decided to "make a positive statement toward life by working in youth ministry."

Dave was also in the Catholic Peace Fellowship and went to meetings with Terry. The group was a coming together of serious-minded people who were committed to peace. Daniel Berrigan once said that those most concerned for the well-being of the future of humanity will find themselves involved in revolution. Pricking the conscience is the business of prophets. A revolution need not be under a barrage of fire, it happens in minds and hearts. "Flower power" was a chant of the antiwar movement.

True prophets have no pat answers, no simplistic solutions. With clear vision, not "visions," they see through the madness of the world's injustices. Clear insight into root problems and intensity of reflection forces them to speak out and to act. In doing so, they give other people reasons to turn toward justice. Terry was convinced that "the message of the gospels does not coincide with the practices of this country both in Southeast Asia and at home."

Terry's concern for peace came from her belief in the gospels and an uncomplicated sensitivity to injustice. She despised oppression, war, and killing. "You just can't condone murder and violence," she said. A sharp awareness of the Vietnam catastrophe made her sympathetic to the peace people; yet, she did not want to get involved in a specific action. The focus of Terry's life was on children and peer ministry. Whatever detracted from that focus, however worthwhile, was a lesser priority. Still a prophet, she stayed close to the group that met in Chuck Hall's apartment.

The draft riled Terry. She saw uneducated black boys

drafted; high-school graduates, too, if they planned no further education. College students were free. The draft was one more inequity in an unholy war.

While Terry and John Nevins were forming a good, lasting friendship, he was not in the peace groups. He probably knew Terry better than any of her friends. The 13 years of his priesthood had been centered on youth; his relaxed appearance and attitude suited him for the work. Terry was an asset and constantly on the Search scene. Possibly, he knew her better than her brothers. When she was hurting, he knew it; however, the comic in Terry usually prevailed. Although she had a good sense of authenticity, he suspected she was being manipulated by some of the people who were in the East Coast Conspiracy. She denied that she was being set up. In the interchange of friendship, she did not use anyone, nor did she expect anyone to use her.

The atmosphere in her apartment changed. Carolyn had reached the painful decision to leave the religious order. She often talked with Terry about wanting to serve but feeling too pressured in a formal religious commitment. She was in the crunch of tensions. In fact, Terry's decision against going to the Notre Dame novitiate was partly influenced by her exposure to the turmoil of people already inside, planning to leave. Terry was edgy in the apartment when Carolyn no longer lived there.

Early in January, 1970 she realized she could not live with Sarah and Pat much longer. She told Pat she "already had a mother." But the peace people intrigued her. There was an air of expectancy when the East Coast Conspiracy met at Chuck's. A mixed bag of emotions drew her into their muted plans for action: adventure, glamor, and the venting of resentment of the war. The odds were against her being reflective and making a cool judgment on her entanglement with the group. They were gentle, loving people. She trusted them.

On a week night, toward the end of the month, one of the group, Tom, asked her to ride around Center City. He came from Boston and wanted to see more of Philadelphia. She drove the van down Broad Street, passed Temple University. It began to snow. City Hall was straight ahead. The yellow face of the City Hall clock glowed. She pointed to places she thought he might want to see: the State building at Springgarden; the Academy of Fine Arts at Broad and Cherry. As they drove around City Hall she made certain he looked up at the statue of Billy Penn on the top of the tower.

"Is it true that no building in the city can be any higher than Billy Penn's hat?" he asked.

"Yeah, how did you know that?"

"Us tourists know more than you natives, sometimes," he teased.

She showed him where she liked to stand to watch the Mummers' Parade on New Year's Day.

Back at Susquehanna Avenue they talked for a while and drank a few beers. He asked her if she would be around any weekend in February.

"You know the flack I get at home about being here on weekends," Terry said. "I was lucky to be able to live here at all. I had to coax my parents to say it was O.K. My dad was not for it, no way."

"But you're almost 20. Why don't you just live where you want?" he asked.

"Well, you know," she said, "we're a pretty close family. I

go along. They even went to see Father Schmidt about me living here. He said that it was really necessary and it would be alright. I'm glad they care. So what, a lot of kids parents don't even care."

"Why did Schmidt think it was necessary?" he asked.

"With the summer programs and all. Tutoring in the winter. It's handy."

She paused for a moment and said, "Besides, I have to check the Search schedule to see what weekends are coming up."

It was not her manner to delve into people's reasons for wanting favors. He pinned it down to one Friday night in particular, then asked if he could borrow the van.

"If I'm here, you'll see the keys," she said.

By coincidence, Terry's sister Carol and her husband came to stay at the house in Overbrook on the weekend in question. The house was near the hospital and their first child was due. Terry gave them her room. Everyone was pleased that Terry could go to the apartment.

Terry and Pat spent a quiet evening listening to Bob Dylan and Joan Baez records. Early Saturday morning Pat was awakened by a noise outside on the street. Looking out the window, she could not see the van. "The van's gone. O my God, the van's gone!" For a minute, she thought Terry had risen early and left but found her still there, asleep. When she stirred, Pat told her the van was not parked out front. Terry bolted up. It should have been there.

She felt the heaviness of responsibility. Clasping her hand over her mouth, she said, "Oh! Oh!" The van was conspicuous with the lettering all over it. And, she was accountable.

They dressed quickly and hurried to the police station to

report the van stolen. After giving information, they turned to leave, thinking that was all. Terry was detained. A rush of feelings made her head spin: first, embarrassment, dread, then a laugh. It was nothing, she thought. It will be cleared up soon. All the while, the police and FBI were searching both apartments at 3007 Susquehanna Avenue.

8. Life, Liberty, and the Pursuit of Happiness

The desert will rejoice, and flowers will bloom in the wastelands.

Isaiah 35:1

Three draft board offices were raided that Friday night in February, 1970. All at the same time. Actually, it was two o'clock on Saturday morning, February 7, when eight people, six men and two women, members of the East Coast Conspiracy to Save Lives, entered the Selective Service headquarters at Broad and Cherry Streets.

During the previous day a group called WAP, Weekly Action Project, sat on the floor, arm-in-arm, to block the entrances to three of the headquarters' offices. The newly-formed coalition planned one antidraft demonstration a week. That day their poster read:

DRAFT BOARD CLOSED BY CITIZENS
TO PROTECT LIFE AND LIBERTY.

When people stepped over their heads to go into the offices the protestors told them they were trying to stop systems that make war possible. An army sergeant wanted to enter and was told, "You're killing people by remote control." Reverend David M. Gracie who led the demonstrators said, "We just want to make people slow down and think it out." Two 18-year-old boys came to register, saw the poster and said, "Cool, let's go home."

In the eerie quiet at 2 a.m., the raiders rifled files and destroyed draft records. They sprayed paper with chlorine and ink eradicator, strewed them on the floor. The headquarters of nine boards was in chaos. A guard spotted them. He went, unnoticed, down the elevator to the lobby, called the police, then returned to the sixth floor. The invaders saw him and ran down a fire escape.

The van sat outside the building. The raiders had driven there from Susquehanna Avenue. All but one scrambled into the van. It refused to start. They ran.

When one of the women spied the guard inside the building, she ducked into the women's room. In the rush to avoid being caught she mistook the word on the door. It was the men's room. The police found her.

Early Saturday morning she was allowed to make one phone call to tell someone that she was in the police station. A stranger to the city, the location meant nothing to her. When she asked the police the address of the station they said the Roundhouse at 8th and Vine. She called the apartment and gave the address to a member of the group. He went to the Roundhouse and asked for his friend. She was not there. He returned to Susquehanna Avenue, not realizing that he was trailed and thereby disclosed the whereabouts of the East Coast Conspiracy. Police and FBI converged on the place with a search warrant.

The other two protest actions of Friday night went off successfully in secret. The Broad and Cherry raiders who had run to the apartment were taken to the police station at 20th and Callowhill. Terry was still there. She pieced things together as they came in.

The security guard easily recognized the woman who had been found hiding. He identified others but was not sure about Terry. She flatly denied being one of the raiding party. Pat, her one reliable back-up had returned to the apartment. A chain of phone calls by police to the Cardinal's Commission, to the Executive Director, to Father Schmidt, led to Terry. She must have been the driver, the police insisted.

Father Schmidt, the McHughs, and Brother Joseph Schmidt, who was principal of West Catholic High School for Boys, came with Father Dowling to be with Terry. A lawyer, Charles Butterworth, was called in by one of the East Coast Conspiracy. Butterworth ran a Catholic Worker Center in a Hispanic neighborhood near 8th and York. As he listened to Terry, he studied her features. He then went to the Youth Study Center (a detention center for young offenders) which was across the street from the police station. He selected four girls who were about the same size as Terry. He managed to get four coats similar to hers. He requested the police to put the girls in a line-up with Terry and have the guard decide if he had seen any one of them the night before. Of course, he could not identify the one. While the rest of the raiders were held for arraignment, Terry was released. She went home with her parents, and within a few hours two FBI men were ringing McHugh's doorbell.

In time, the turmoil surrounding the raids subsided. It was the unhappy start, however, of months of stress for Terry that would lead to a crisis of fright. When the FBI men came to the house in Overbrook on Saturday afternoon, her parents spoke freely although Terry was noncommital. She was asked to come to the Center City FBI office on Monday for questioning. When the men left, she told her parents she did not plan to go in, hoping to end the situation that easily.

After supper Saturday evening she went to Cardinal Krol's residence on City Line Avenue, not far from her house. The large gray turreted house sits on an expanse of lawn. Fences and shrubbery along City Avenue seclude it. The flat curving driveway leads to a porte cochere. A sister who answered the door told Terry the cardinal was not at home. She sat on the step, waiting, until the winter night chilled her through. On Sunday she returned and was told he was not at home. Ready for a longer vigil, she bundled in warm clothing and waited again. Her remorse over getting Fathers Schmidt and Dowling in serious trouble over the van forced her to try to cut around protocol. There was an urgency in her need to explain the circumstances to the cardinal so that the priests would not be blamed. But she was not given the chance to talk with him.

The atmosphere at home was stilted. Marge and Bud McHugh were faced with a gap in the relationship with their daughter. Thinking they were privileged counselors to their children, they were jolted by the incident that made Terry a stranger. In their view, the authority of government was sacrosanct. They respected, and were respected by, others who thought the same. Their children cooperated and, they hoped, espoused the same standards. Generous, open-hearted warmth, braced with a readiness to celebrate, mellowed the heaviness of control. The family was a loving community, with it all. And the house was a party place on holidays. While they tolerated differing opinions about the war, they regarded open protest as distasteful, in fact, disloyal. Bud McHugh served in the Second World War willingly. In the 25 years since then, his patriotism had not wavered and the FBI had always been a symbol of high integrity and efficiency. Terry's flagrant antiwar attitude conflicted with her parents' stance. Furthermore, her association with the East Coast Conspiracy widened the breach. Their love, both Terry's and her parent's, was severely tested and, in the testing, strengthened.

Terry moved the last of her belongings from the apartment, but she did not break her ties with the neighborhood. The children who knew what had happened were bewildered. Terry and Joe Corley planned to continue the summer programs elsewhere. Sarah and Pat left the apartment when the diocese clamped down on sisters residing in a place that spawned the raid of a draft board.

Bud McHugh gave Terry no choice when it came time to go to the FBI for questioning. Terry's lawyer, Burton Caine, advised her to say nothing. She was pleasant and politely declined to answer.

Leaving the house for work one morning, Bud McHugh noticed two men in a car parked across the street. As he drove up Wynnewood Road, he saw the car swing around and follow him. Shortly, another car parked in its place; two men glanced at the house every so often. When Terry came out, they followed her. Whenever she drove her father to work, they trailed the car. McHugh's phone conversations were interrupted by a sharp crackling sound. Friends who called complained of hearing the loud click. Some people whose names were on the Cursillo list heard the noise on their phones even though they were not calling McHughs. Terry's attorney made a phone call to a client from his office, hung up, then lifted the receiver to dial again and heard his previous conversation played back. The FBI had begun its surveillance.

Sometimes when Terry saw the parked car in the morning, she walked over to the agents and asked if they wanted a cup of coffee. Her offer was not defiant but genuinely considerate. At other times, before she got in the family car, she went to the men and told them where she was going. "First, I'm stopping for doughnuts, then I'm driving my Dad to work, then I'm going to school." For her, it's true, there was a tinge of humor in sticking a pin in their balloon. Terry ran a few yards ahead of life's grind.

To some extent she lost contact with high-school friends. For one thing, they called less often and she sensed a coolness. It seemed pushy to pursue them. A few were outright resentful of her identity with antiwar groups. To be with her and be trailed by FBI was expecting too much. They could not cope. For instance, one friend, Janey, made sure that Terry knew she was one of the silent majority. "Nothing is gained by demonstrating," she argued, "the middle generation is disturbed by it. It doesn't change a thing."

Bud McHugh's relatives and friends kept their distance. No one called to support them when news of Terry's predicament spread. The unwillingness to understand, the show of disapproval by silence persisted throughout the duration of the surveillance. At that time, there was no way of knowing how long it would go on. Neither did anyone know exactly why the FBI would not let Terry out of their sight. No charge had been made. Her only implication in the raid on the draft board was that she was responsible for the van that someone else used. The tenor of the government at the time, even in the White House, suggested a paranoia regarding the Catholic Left—the most vigorous and most articulate effort against the Vietnam war. The delusion also made young people who were involved in youth and peace work suspect. Terry's lawyer speculates that the government agents wanted to wear Terry down so that she would give them information about people and plans. Her young age was in their favor, perhaps. They did not know that while Terry quaked with fear and doubt, she made her decisions based on her own convictions. For Marge and Bud McHugh, the community of their home boosted their morale. Their first grandchild, Carol and Jay's new daughter, brought much needed joy.

Father Schmidt never flinched during the van episode. CSC personnel and programs remained valid. The March issue of *The Hint,* the CSC–CYO newspaper, carried a statement by Father Schmidt:

> Individual members of CSC are free to have varying degrees of sympathy for those whose consciences lead them to various acts of civil disobedience. However, it is and always will be the style of the CSC organization and official representatives to work within the structure.

Support came anonymously when several diocesan priests sent money to Father Schmidt for Terry's legal fees. It was not needed because Burton Caine accepted no money.

The priest who was principal of St. Maria Goretti High School in South Philadelphia told Father Schmidt, "I would like to boast that she has graduated from here, but alas, this is the distinction of West Catholic."

It bothered Terry to see her dad trailed, knowing how

he felt about the FBI and their glory. She felt sad about the family, not hearing from friends and the relatives staying away. She imagined the agents trying to talk to her younger sisters. Helene was eight and Joanne was only five years old. That was scary. And to make it worse, mealtimes were heavy. Everyone felt the strain. Conversations seemed artificial sometimes. And in laughter she thought she heard shouts of resentment. If she could have gone to the front door and yelled, "Hey you guys, bug off," and the unmarked car would skulk away, maybe she could be more at ease in the house. "It was a worrying time," Marge McHugh says, "more worry than anything else."

Search weekends were a haven for Terry. Search had become popular and summer weekends were planned. The facilities at Neumann, however, were not available. It was a summer camp for children. When Father Nevins celebrated Mass with the Medical Mission Sisters in Fox Chase, he eyed an empty house on their property. It fronted Pine Road in northeast Philadelphia and was for sale. While it remained idle, he asked if he could use it for Search weekends. The sisters agreed. He told Terry about his "find" and took her to see it. More grandiose than Camp Neumann, it was secluded and spacious.

"The sisters have places at the shore," he told Terry, "I'm pretty sure they'll let us hold Searches there too."

Jack Nevins, for all his two score years, looked boyish. His six-foot frame seemed ready to take the ball down the court gracefully. While most sports people wear Adidas or facsimiles, Nevins wears basketball sneakers and sweat socks. His conversation is interspersed with quick laughs, although in his liturgies he moves slowly and seems to caress the words.

"You must know the boss here," Terry said.

"Oh, it isn't that so much. These nuns are all for the Search kind of thing. They love good liturgy and all that."

He saw Terry look toward the driveway and scan Pine Road. "Expecting somebody?" he asked.

"I can't believe it. I mean it's really unreal," she started to laugh, waving her arms out and then down to a big clap. "They didn't follow us. We lost them. Ha!"

She told him about the surveillance and her decision to live somewhere else. "I have no car. The only money I have comes from summer work in CSC and I know it's better that I get out of the house." She merely stated facts.

"Stay here," he said.

"What, you gotta be kidding."

"It looks to me as if you can live here. Why not? I'll talk to the superior and tell her what's going on. I'm trying to work something else out here anyway, so I've gotten to know her. This place would be good for kids who are into drugs—sort of a rehab center. It's in the sticks, no stores around. Frank Schmidt says drugs are becoming a big problem with kids and Pete Quinn is dying to get a place started so he can help them."

"But it's for sale."

"Yes, but Pete will probably get funding to buy it. I don't see why you can't stay here until we see what happens."

No one had followed them. No one saw them leave. Terry had found a sanctuary.

Pine Road is one of the last country roads in the city. It winds through pastures and parks. In this rural setting the headquarters of the worldwide activities of the Society of Catholic Medical Missionaries is located. Terry moved into the old white house near the entrance. A winding driveway passes several "cottages," new residences of the sisters. Farther into the woods a summer-type house called the Boathouse edges a clearing of grass that might have been a lake, but never was. Sisters who return from serving in foreign countries come to Pine Road to be reoriented to American culture.

Their penchant for recognizing the needs of people in their environment led the sisters to open the door in 1968 to neighbors who wanted to share the Sunday liturgy. Sunday Mass at the Medical Missions was intimate and meaningful. As a young father of two children put it, "Going to Sunday Mass at the parish is like being in a 747 aircraft hanger, I feel so removed from the liturgy." On most Sundays, there was standing room only in the chapel. While Terry lived there, typically, she became a vital part of the worshiping community.

While he was eluding the FBI, Daniel Berrigan wrote about pursuit: "Those who pursue happiness must endure unhappiness, the dark night of resistance, doubt, delusion, nightmare, because they pursue decency and a human future for the despised and expendable, the wretched of the earth."

Terry endured unhappiness and found a place that evaded the pursuers. Some say that living at the Medical Missions was a desert experience for Terry, meaning that she needed the separateness to replenish her spirit. The desert blooms in spring and the air is scented with the perfume of blossoms. Being drawn to the Medical Mission Sisters, to live on the fringe of their community, ended Terry's winter somewhat. She needed time for newness. Underneath a gregarious and high spirit, Terry was a private person.

Enduring the dark night of resistance, her commitment to protest the war deepened. Along with friends in the peace community she endured the nightmare of the shootings at Kent State. She put herself in the place of those students in Ohio. There had been wanton destruction in the town of Kent and the National Guard was called in to quell disturbances. Contradictions between statements from the White House and news releases from Vietnam sent Kent State University protestors on a rampage. On April 30, American forces attacked Cambodia. The hysteria of destruction in Kent, however, went beyond the bounds of legitimate protest. Emotions rode high. While students noisily protested the invasion of Cambodia by meeting on campus during the day, May 4, the Guard opened fire on the unarmed people. Four died.

Terry evaded the FBI, temporarily. Agents questioned her parents, Father Schmidt, and CSC friends, trying to locate her. Eventually, her pursuers connected with Pine Road. Terry was busy preparing the house for Search weekends when her friend Marie Forish came one afternoon. They drove to Camp Neumann for supplies, stopping at a snack stand for a coke. Marie saw a Volkswagen drive behind them and stop. When Terry waved her hand in a "don't bother" gesture, Marie looked puzzled. Terry said, "Oh, they're those two guys who are trailing me." Going over to the VW she asked, "Do you want us to get you a soda?" They said, "No thanks," staring straight ahead. The girls started to laugh. For the pursued there is a time to worry, a time to laugh, and a time to flee.

Later in the summer, John Nevins held Search weekends in the Medical Mission house at Avalon. Again, Terry was the key member of the team. Agents sat in a parked car, watching the house and the beach. Feeling much the same as when she was first trailed at home, Terry was reluctant to have Search hounded by the FBI. Her heart was in the program but her consideration for others prompted her to be less involved.

The summer programs established at The Shoppe in previous summers continued at the house on Pine Road. Joe Corley and other CSC people transported children. Open fields were a relief from the hot asphalt of north Philadelphia. Kids rolled on the ground to feel and smell the grass. It was a completely new experience for some of them. When they played baseball, Terry coached with the intensity of Casey Stengel. Then, to quiet down, they sat in a circle in the shade of an old oak and sang: "This land is your land," and "He's got the whole world in his hands." Invariably, the children would sing, "He's got Terry McHugh in his hands."

9. Riding the Crest

> *He sets the time for sorrow and the
> time for joy, He sets the time for find-
> ing and the time for losing.*
>
> Ecclesiastes 3:4,6

The FBI's surveillance of Terry would have persisted even if she had submitted to questioning. Innumerable peace people were trailed. Their phones crackled. Terry, however, was tracked down more than any of her friends and associates.

Jeanne Walsh was followed. For a while, agents parked outside the inner-city school where she taught. Her phone was bugged. She knew in her bones that the American military presence in Vietnam was wrong, immoral. She did not pay the federal tax on her telephone bill because the tax money went for military spending. Jeanne first heard of Terry when news of the van being used in the draft board raid spread through the peace-community network. She shared Terry's empathy for inner-city poor and disgust for war. Naturally, their friendship grew quickly. Terry's attentive blue eyes made Jeanne, and many others, feel "that there was something real close inside that rarely happens with anyone else."

Jeanne lived near Terry's family in Overbrook. When Terry stopped at home, once in a while she rode around the corner to chat. Jeanne needed a friend who saw what she saw. Happily, Terry had a way of dropping in at the precise time when Jeanne felt the need to talk about her doubts and concerns. Terry had the ability to be present. As she listened, her thoughts were nowhere else. She made you think you were the only person in the world. They sat on the back steps for a long time one evening. After the usual small talk, they got to the issues that burned at the center of their lives. Jeanne was wondering whether or not it was worth staying in the inner-city school.

"I'm drained. Should I go on being drained? I'll be a social ministry drop-out. Come on, Terry, give me answers."

Terry listened; said nothing.

"I see children come in to the classroom wiped out by the age of eight," Jeanne continued, "and there's nothing to get them going. I know I have to stay with them, then I have no energy left."

"You feel you're their only hope?"

"Yeah, and it's heavy," Jeanne said. "I see money being pumped into a big military build-up and into all the corporations that tie into it, then very little comes into the poor areas. Those kids are wasted. There are a lot of doubts going through my head."

"I know what you mean," Terry agreed.

Jeanne went on. "Government allows decay and subhuman conditions to go on. It allows a ghetto and it allows a war, different realities from the same source."

"You can't be hurting about the poor and not be hurting about the war," Terry said. She suffered the same frustration. She knew how things *should* be and tried to deal with them as they were.

"You know something could be done," Jeanne was emphatic, "if brains were put into it. Something could be done."

Anger and spiritual burn-out result from involvement in social justice ministry. The work among the poor simply draws out the anger and anti-authoritarian elements that are present in most people. Whatever the source, anger and burn-out are realities for most activists. They are potentially self-destructive. To survive, then, is to be aware of all that pushes anger to the surface, deal with it positively and creatively.

They talked about the Beatitudes, about the basic strength they found in them.

"They're the closest answer," Terry said. "We have to be our own witness."

When there were no Search weekends at Pine Road, Terry went to the house at Avalon. She slipped away through back roads or on the floor in the back of a friend's car. The surveillance was nerve-racking. Feeling hounded, she needed time away from the agents' scrutiny. She feared their next move, not really knowing if or when she would be confronted by them. An affluent, residential resort, Avalon's wide beach stretches seven miles and sweeps up to an untouched, natural preserve of dunes. Terry was in awe of their rugged beauty. Once there and undetected, she hid with the help of a priest she knew from Search, Father Vincent DiPasquale. He brought her food. He also put her to work training Search teams for the South Jersey area. Terry helped him run Searches in the house for the students he taught. Vince was also assistant pastor in an Atlantic City parish, indirectly involved in the peace movement.

He thought the war was immoral. The FBI trailed him,

perhaps because he went to a couple East Coast Conspiracy meetings. More likely, it was a result of entertaining Phil Berrigan and friends in Atlantic City one weekend. "It was just a chance for them to rest at the shore," he said, "Terry introduced me to them. And for that, I get trailed."

Father DiPasquale redesigned his Search program. It ended at eleven Sunday morning. From one to five he had a re-entry session. "Too many kids were getting strung out," he says. "They were getting hurt by hitting the wall after the euphoria of the weekend. The kids were all hyped up over Jesus, but on Monday morning they'd try to tell kids at school about Jesus and they'd get laughed at." He prepared them for a more moderate but longer-lasting joy in the Lord.

Vince believes that despite her hearty laugh Terry was enduring a dark night of doubt and delusion. In the post-raid period, being trailed became adventurous, even funny at times. Vince thought Terry was melodramatic. "A little bit of the kid was still in her. Basically, Terry operated from a belief in the gospel," Vince says. "She lived it."

He realized that she was a sensitive, beautiful person, a bit of a poet. It was unusual for a person her age to have a mature faith, a real sense of the gospel.

"She was a ray of hope in a garbage can," he says. "I knew the street ways. I was the realist, always battling institutions and systems. She'd come off with this gospel stuff. She was very familiar with it and kept saying 'You've got to be positive like putting on the new man and all that.' I'd say, 'It's O.K., Terry, but it doesn't work.'"

"Damn, how can you say that?"

Vince had been ordained four years. Whether or not his ideals were tarnished in disillusion is anybody's guess. He dealt with stark reality and the message of the gospel was an ideal to uphold but not a reality to be lived.

"I'm going to give you a copy of *The Gospel According to Peanuts*," Terry told him.

"Now you want me to read comic books."

"I'm serious. It puts St. James in plain language," she said.

"Terry, if you take it literally, you get used. People take advantage. Like you and some of the East Coast Conspiracy people. They used you to get places to live. Here, for instance. You wait, they'll come to Pine Road, too. Terry better take care of Terry."

He thought Terry was gullible at times, and probably she was.

Certainly, she was misunderstood. Some people thought she was a wild kid who thrived on being chased, a little crazy. She persevered through misunderstanding; if given a chance, she would have consoled people who held those thoughts. She exuded energy and was ready for anything daring.

"You're riding the crest of the wave," Vince told her, "and when you come flyin' down, you're going to come crashing."

It took Vince another seven years to understand what Terry meant by living the gospel. It was woven into her life, so, it was natural to get involved in working to change anything that was contrary. Moreover, she was exceptionally bright, according to Vince. When she went back to Temple "she didn't really have to sit in a classroom to handle that stuff."

The house on Pine Road was in the process of becoming a live-in rehabilitation residence for young drug users. The Bridge, it was called. Terry moved into House #6, one of the sisters' cottages. She biked to Temple. The pesky writing problem resumed its place of contention. Getting the words through her head onto the paper was a struggle. John Nevins, who saw her more consistently than anyone else, noticed that she paused in the middle of a conversation, in the middle of a phrase, as if to gather her thoughts and express them clearly. Even so, her classes went well. Vince DiPasquale's evaluation of her intelligence was on target.

Sure enough, eight of Terry's friends from the East Coast Conspiracy took up lodging in the chaplain's quarters on Pine Road. They stayed six months. During that time, Dorothy Ann Klein, superior of the sisters, attended a conference in Washington, D.C. on Latin America. It contrasted the "haves" and the "have-nots," showing the shocking difference between northern American societies and poverty-ridden Mexico. The conference shook Dorothy Ann to the core. She, and two other sisters, decided to move out of the semi-opulence of Pine Road into an old rowhouse in a run-down section of Germantown. Terry went with them. It was similar to the Susquehanna environment. The new residents of 123 Apsley Street were a community of four; they prayed together each day.

Terry made a point of meeting the children of the neighborhood. Knowing her way around City Hall, she obtained a permit to close off Apsley Street for a block party. She got the wrench for the fire hydrant so kids could splash in warm weather. Befriending the black teenagers, she soon learned that there were no recreation facilities near their homes. Terry and Dorothy Ann put a make-shift ping pong table in the basement, and a group of boys used it regularly.

The small Medical Mission community was settled in the

house a short time when Dorothy Ann, better known as "D.A.," became aware of Terry's involvement in the peace movement.

Terry contributed a few dollars a month toward household expenses with money she received from working on Search. Although more of a consultant than a regular team leader, she was asked to work on a special weekend for a racially mixed group from both West Catholic high schools, girls and boys. When the team met for a briefing in advance, Terry met John Devenney. At first he was beguiled by her perky look in a tan knit beret. A colorful hand-knit poncho set off her fair complexion. They stood for a moment and saw a welcome in each other's eyes. Simpatico. They had much in common. Both were in college, although John was at Penn State. They were the same age, deeply involved in a sense of commitment to the needs of other people, especially their peers. John's sensitive brown eyes warmed Terry, gave her a feeling of peace and security.

On the weekend, the sessions were hectic. Racial conflicts flared and the team's patience frayed. After the kids went to their cabins for the night, John and Terry took a long walk down a lane. They talked about the impermanence in their lives. So much had changed in just a few years. In the still of the night, under an autumn sky, they knew their friendship was no longer casual. It grew deeper and closer.

The next morning Terry told John she had had a startling dream. Everyone she knew was chasing her through the woods. The only one she could run to, and be safe, was John. From then on, they would sneak away to be together, growing closer all the time.

Terry was aware that their relationship could be a problem at that time in their lives. John knew it, too. They were afraid of anything that smacked of permanence. A distrust of permanence had already begun to cut across the young-adult population. It was a symptom of a continuing malaise of the times. Both Terry and John wanted to finish college. Surveillance was a hindrance to Terry. And through it all an unclear, unresolved desire to be part of the Medical Mission community nagged at her.

They saw each other on weekends at Neumann. When the clamor quieted down, they sat by the fireplace and talked. Or, Bob McCarty would go with them for pizza and beer. They became a trio and sometimes ended a day by walking in the woods. It was quite natural to share prayer, open the Bible at random and talk about what it meant in their lives.

During the Thanksgiving holiday, John helped Terry prepare a party for the neighbors on Apsley Street. D.A. had decided that an open-house was the appropriate way to let people know they were approachable. The party went well. However, in a few days a guest, who was a deputy sheriff, stormed up to their front door and demanded to know, "Who are you, *really?*" The FBI had badgered him, wanting to know what he and the others were doing in that house. The landlord did not want his house under question by the FBI, and he threatened to evict them until D.A. explained that it was a satellite convent.

Until then, Terry was not aware that the house was watched. She was dismayed when she learned that her parents had given the FBI her address. To the McHughs, it seemed only right.

"They were told they would not be bothered, and I would simply be questioned," Terry told D.A. "So they did it thinking they were doing the right thing. The FBI has been calling them and coming to the house ever since. The phone still sounds like it's bugged."

Harassment was the word Terry used for the FBI's unrelenting surveillance.

After dinner on an evening in April, Terry answered a knock on the door. A man asked for Theresa McHugh. "What do you want her for?" she asked.

"I have to deliver this." He held an envelope.

"I'll give it to her," she said.

"No, I have to hand it to her personally," he insisted.

"O.K. That's my name. I'll take it."

The envelope contained a subpoena. Terry was called to testify before the federal grand jury convened to hear charges brought by the U.S. government against Philip Berrigan and several others accused of plotting to kidnap Henry Kissinger, at that time the president's security adviser, and to blow up the heating systems in Washington.

"So, it's come to this." Terry slumped in a chair. "Damn! Testify. It calls me a 'witness.' Witness to what? What do they want me for? What a hell of a mess."

Terry showed D.A. the subpoena. "If I say anything at all, it'll open up a lousy can of worms. Hell can freeze over before I'll say anything that'll turn anybody in."

Terry called her lawyer, Burton Caine. He told her to honor the subpoena. She said that she did not want to testify. He advised her that silence could result in a jail sentence. She was due to testify in a week. Burton Caine encouraged her to refuse to incriminate anyone from the witness stand. The Constitution was in her favor and he planned to prove it.

Nevertheless, the thought of going to jail horrified her. She bore the prospect patiently and, after the shock of the subpoena, seemed calm.

When she told John Devenney, a smile was on her lips, but not in her eyes. She talked about the tensions of the weeks, maybe months, ahead.

"If we promise too much to each other and I go to jail, you'll be alone. It doesn't seen fair to you." Terry said.

For her own part, she was afraid jail would change her; she would be hardened. Courage is one thing, callousness quite another.

"Terry, we have to wait to see what comes of all this. Let's put our relationship on 'hold,'" John said.

Tears came to her eyes. They both cried.

About seven in the morning, April 19, Father Nevins drove Terry the hundred miles to Harrisburg, Pa., where the federal grand jury was meeting. Sisters Pat and Sarah and Father DiPasquale were among 32 subpoenaed witnesses. Burton Caine briefed Terry outside the courtroom as the gavel pounded.

10. Ritual of Refusal

In the broadest sense, there is no Christian who is not a minister of the gospel.
A Vision of Youth Ministry
U.S. Catholic Conference

Peace people milled around the entrance to the courthouse, a ten-story glass and steel building in downtown Harrisburg. Some wanted to show support of the defendants and witnesses by their presence; others tried to get into the courtroom to hear the proceedings first hand. The judge was R. Dixon Herman, known less formally as "Hanging Herman." The nickname indicated local opinion of his decisions. In addition to the jury, three U.S. attorneys were present. The defense attorneys were not permitted inside the courtroom. Prosecuting attorneys, alone, questioned defendants and witnesses. On the first day they were called, Terry and all others were asked their names and addresses and then told to return the next day. She met her parents and Joanne who were in the corridor. They drove two hundred miles back and forth each day of the hearings. At first Marge and Bud McHugh were non-judgmental, then supportive of Terry. John McNamee accompanied them. Marge tried to buoy spirits while Terry remained outwardly calm and passive. Later, she confided to Jeanne Walsh, who came when she could, "I'm terrified."

In January of 1971, Philip Berrigan and five others had been indicted by the federal grand jury meeting in Harrisburg. Seven others, including Daniel Berrigan, were named as unindicted co-conspirators. One of the co-conspirators, Sister Jogues Egan, was also cited for contempt for refusing to testify even though promised immunity.

All of those charged had been active in the antiwar movement. It was alleged that they planned to use the kidnapping of Henry Kissinger and the blowing up of the heating systems of five federal buildings as a way to force the Nixon administration to stop the bombing of Vietnam and Cambodia.

The defendants and their supporters vigorously denied the government's charges. They pointed out that the kind of violent action they were being accused of was exactly the kind of thing they were protesting against. It seemed to many that an attempt was being made by the administration to intimidate and suppress the entire peace movement, and one of the defendants' lawyers, William Kunstler, drew a comparison with the suppression of public protest in Nazi Germany.

Thirty-eight years ago, the Nazi party burnt the Reichstag in order to stampede the German people into supporting a policy of repression at home and militarism abroad. The government of the United States, for much the same purpose, has created a grotesque conspiracy to kidnap a presidential assistant and blow up the heating systems of federal buildings in Washington. The objective is a simple but deadly one: to destroy the peace movement by creating caricatures of those who oppose the war in Southeast Asia.

Burton Caine said that the alleged plot was "the most fanciful fairy tale I have ever heard, utterly preposterous." People he knew who were subpoened were open and loving and could not have conceived such an intricate scenario.

The defendants and co-conspirators issued a public statement protesting the actions of the government:

> It is the government which has not only conspired but carried out the destruction by explosives of three countries: Vietnam, Laos, and Cambodia, crippling these defenseless people with napalm and pellet bombs, destroying their forests and rice fields. If one is concerned with crimes against humanity, it is the officials of the U.S. government who should be on trial. . . . The atmosphere of intimidation created by the grand jury, which began historically as a shield to protect the innocent . . . has become instead a sword to oppress the defenseless.

Following the arraignment of the Harrisburg Six, as those indicted came to be known, the grand jury continued to hear witnesses as the justice department attempted to find evidence of criminal activity by the various antiwar groups.

Terry's association with peace activists obviously made her a possible source of information. In her second appearance before the grand jury, she was the first witness to be called. She was unusually young to be deeply committed to the peace movement, the youngest witness to be called and, because of her youth, vulnerable. It was an added burden to be the first witness that day; she did not know what to expect. Outside the courtroom, her attorney coached her in ways to phrase objections to questions and ask to seek advice of counsel.

The government's attorney questioned her. She refused to answer, objecting to the question on the grounds of her constitutional rights. Specifically, the fourth and fifth amendments.

The fourth amendment protects people from illegal search and seizure. Terry believed the FBI had tried to obtain evidence by the illegal use of electronic surveillance —wiretapping. The fifth amendment protects people from incriminating themselves. She did not want to accuse herself or any other person who was innocent.

Seven witnesses, through their lawyers, tried to have their subpoenas quashed, declaring the government was involved in illegal wiretapping. Litigations in other courts went on simultaneously in efforts to negate subpoenas. Sister Jogues Egan, who had been sentenced to jail for her refusal to testify, was released without bail while her case was being appealed to the Supreme Court. Some charged that the continued activity of the grand jury after it had handed down indictments was an abuse of its authority. Not all witnesses were called to testify. Father Vince Di-Pasquale, for instance. Others answered a few questions, waited in the hallway and were not called again.

Terry's lawyer and John McNamee surmised that the government lawyers would call Terry repeatedly in an effort to chip away at her determination. When she was called the third time, she was offered immunity. She could return home free if she answered questions. The glimpse at freedom had limits. Immune questions pertained to the original indictment only: the plot. Many other questions could be asked. Even though she was not involved in the alleged plot, her courtroom naivete would serve the purposes of the prosecution. She refused immunity and, thereby, was in contempt of court. The penalty: incarceration in a federal prison for the duration of the grand jury. It could last a year or more.

Terry was called to the witness stand several times and persevered in a ritual of refusal. She told John Nevins as they returned to Philadelphia late one afternoon: "I think the government is out to get those people and is deliberately trying to convict them before there is any real evidence, and I don't want to be a part of that."

"You're pretty sure of that," he said. "That's heavy. We were sweating it out while you were in the courtroom. Your mother was on pins and needles. What was it like in there?"

"Lonely. Awful. Now I know how Jesus felt."

Driving east on the turnpike, they were quiet for a while. Terry looked out at fields turning green. Trees on a hillside brown-gray, were budding.

John Nevins' concern was for Terry. He was a totally fair man; still, the progress of the peace people did not consume him. Rather, Terry's peace and her future were foremost, and he thought of little else during the hearings.

"Cheer up, we'll be playing tennis again this summer," he said.

"Yeah, at Muncie."

"Why don't you make reservations at the Allenwood prison, they have an executive golf course there," he teased.

Father Nevins is a people person. His subtle affirmation makes his young friends solid as a rock. When his banter seems trivial, all the while he conveys a resounding "yes" to their gifts and hopes.

The trial stayed on Terry's mind as they sped toward home. "I don't believe what they're doing is right. They are overruling all our legal rights, and if we let them they'll keep doing it. It's a good thing this is a big case and it's getting lots of attention."

She went on giving vent to the turmoil pent up within. "Most of these people haven't set out to destroy anything. They've tried to continue life and that's what it's all about. Damn! They go by concern for human life. That's what's important."

Terry did not want to implicate people who were not guilty of a crime but who might be hassled. She was willing to go to jail simply because she did not want to get other people into trouble.

Meanwhile, Burton Caine continually made legal presentations on Terry's behalf to the U.S. District Court. He tried to get her subpoena canceled, declaring it was based on illegal wiretapping by the government. Wiretapping in the interest of national security was legal, providing a court approved its use. Caine's goal was to prove the FBI had bugged the phones without court approval.

He asked the attorney general to personally investigate the possibility of the existence of wiretapping. An affidavit from the attorney general came to him at the District Court denying any "unlawful wiretapping." Caine objected that the FBI had not asked for or received clearance to use electronic surveillance. When he asked government attorneys in court to clearly admit or deny wiretapping, they told the judge, "We don't care to respond."

The hearings continued on into May. One weekend in May Terry went to an antiwar protest rally in Washington, D.C. Emotionally, she was trying to prepare herself for the prison experience which might be imminent. She was shocked at what happened in Washington, and it frightened her all the more. On the way to Harrisburg Monday morning, she told John Nevins she could not believe the number of people who were taken to jail from the rally.

"I saw people behind barbed wire. The police had trucks the size of tractor trailers set up like prisons. Jack, I've never seen people clubbed except on television."

"Yeah? Didn't you take a chance going? I should know better than to ask." He glanced at her face, flushed with anger. Then he noticed her voice regain composure.

She went through the grand jury questioning with a smile, raised her hand in a peace sign to friends outside the courthouse. Her shoulders hunched, slightly, and her back slumped when she was under tension. Those who knew her well detected stress.

Interest in the proceedings mounted daily as more people gathered outside the building. They sang folk songs and Terry often lingered, joining them. Feelings flared one day. The gathering became unruly. She stood on the courthouse steps and began to sing "We Shall Overcome." She beckoned for people to sing; guitarists strummed the chords. Soon everyone was singing and the uproar, whatever the reason, subsided.

"You have to realize what a rare person she was," says Burton Caine. "She just returned love for hate and for every cruelty, she was kind. It was very clear, not only to me, but to everybody who saw her that she was a ray of sunshine on a stormy day.

"She wore her colorful hat and poncho. Everybody was gloomy because the government was so heavy-handed, so nefarious. Everybody walked in there with a frown. Terry was one who had a big, broad smile, was cheering us all up."

The crowd outside the courthouse formed a human chain one afternoon, linking hands, encircling the entire building. They intended to prevent anyone from entering. Police disbanded the chain and the protesters were corralled in the Farm Show Arena. Neither fined nor jailed, over three hundred people were released in a few hours.

The meaning of the crisis in Terry's life became clearer as the possibility of prison came closer. Few precious days were left to be with her family. The prospect of parting from Joanne made her feel sick. A poor model for a little sister, she thought. Few nights left to open a six-pack with friends and listen to their summer plans. Her guards will wear uniforms; their guards will be in swim trunks, have deep tans and whistle at the girls on the beach. School will stop for her. "Will I want to go back?" she wondered. Then there were the kids around Apsley Street and 29th and Susquehanna. Too familiar with seeing their older brothers and sisters go to jail, it became a status symbol in their perspective. Now, they will not understand. She will lose them. She groped for brighter thoughts.

"Jack Nevins will come to see me, I'm sure. And the food, yuk. No burgers and fries. No pizza and beer. Oh, they'll have oatmeal, but not like Mom's. I bet you'll be able to lay bricks with it."

Her ritual of refusing to testify had strengthened her and brought the joy that comes with knowing what you are doing is right. But anxiety was also there.

Burton Caine presented character witnesses, attempting to mollify Judge Herman's decision. Dr. Frances Van-Divier, director of the child-care program at Temple University, came prepared to tell how she admired Terry's way with children. Father Gerard Sloyan, from Temple's religion department upheld Terry's good reputation. Finally, Father Schmidt was called as a friend and priest to give his moral interpretation of Terry's refusal to testify.

Father Schmidt stands a strapping six feet plus tall. His deep, low voice connotes patience. The gravity of a bespectacled, ruddy face lightens in a quick, hearty laugh. His leadership of youth is one of influence and respect rather than denigrating control. A loving community formed around him and Terry was part of it. He told the grand jury that Terry's refusal to answer questions "indicated the highest moral principles as she sees them. Her convictions make her obey the law of God."

As the hearings continued, Terry labored over composing a statement, struggling to organize her thoughts on paper. She wanted her beliefs to flow out to the judge and jury. When they heard her values, perhaps they would understand. She was called to the witness stand and read the statement slowly, with self-assurance:

A world without violence is an ideal. But that does not mean that we should reject the ideal and be satisfied with the real world. We might never attain our ideal, but only in choosing life can we begin to make peace. And in the end we will be judged not by whether we attained the ideal, but by how well we tried.

We are faced daily with destruction and death in our cities, oppression of the poor, hunger and repeated acts of our inhumanity to man. It is rare that we find people who have such love that they are willing to lay down their lives for their friends. They should not be condemned but praised for choosing life.

Therefore, I take a stand in support of all people opposed to violence, and I say YES to their lives.

Choose life, then, so that you and your descendants may live, in the love of Yahweh your God, obeying his voice, clinging to him; for in this your life consists. (I Dt. 30:20)

We ourselves have known and put faith in God's love towards ourselves. God is love and anyone who lives in love lives in God, and God lives in him. Love will come to its perfection in us when we can face the day of Judgment without fear, because even in this world we have become as He is. In love there can be no fear, but fear is driven out by perfect love: because to fear is to expect punishment, and anyone who is afraid is still imperfect in love. We are to love, then, because he loved us first. Anyone who says, "I love God," and hates his brother, is a liar, since a man who does not love the brother that he can see, cannot love God, whom he has never seen. So this is the commandment that he has given us, that anyone who loves God must also love his brother. (I Jn. 4:16-21)

"How happy are you who are poor: yours is the Kingdom of God.

Happy you who are hungry now: you shall be satisfied.

Happy you who weep now: you shall laugh.

Happy are you when people hate you, drive you out, abuse you, denounce your name as criminal, on account of the Son of Man. Rejoice when that day comes and dance for joy, for then your reward will be great in heaven." (Lk. 6:20-23)

And may the peace of Christ reign in your hearts, because it is for this that you were called together as parts of one body. (Col. 3:15)

Be compassionate as Your Father is compassionate. Do not judge, and you will not be judged yourselves; do not condemn, and you will not be condemned yourselves; grant pardon, and you will be pardoned. (Lk. 6:36-37)

Do all you can to live at peace with everyone. (Rom. 12:18)

Everyone has to do his part to stop the violence. *In the spirit of love, I urge you* to do so.

The court accepted two petitions on behalf of Terry. One from Cardinal Dougherty High School carrying more than 50 signatures of students and faculty members; the other signed by 63 faculty members from Temple University and supported by the student senate.

The Temple petition read: "We do not feel she should be cited for contempt. Before the grand jury she stated, 'It is rare that we find people who have such love that they are willing to lay down their lives for their friends. They should not be condemned, but praised for choosing life.' We believe this applies to Theresa herself."

On May 12, the judge ordered Terry to begin a term in a federal prison.

Burton Caine immediately took her case into the Third Circuit Court of Appeals, arguing the sentence should be suspended on the grounds of illegal wiretapping. It was stayed while the appeal was being considered. The Appeals Court judge set May 28 as the date a decision would be rendered.

On the Sunday before the crucial day, the sisters in the house on Apsley Street gave Terry a farewell party, an open house. Terry's friends from CSC, Search, and the peace movement packed the place. Granting some solemnity to the occasion, she wore a dress instead of the usual dungarees. Terry and Pat St. Clair left the buzz of dangling conversations and sat quietly, somewhat sadly, in Terry's room talking about the awesome tomorrows.

During the course of the appeal, the U.S. Supreme Court reached a decision in the wiretapping case brought by Sister

Jogues Egan. The Court held that if there is a suspicion that the identity of the witness or other material aspects of her background were obtained by wiretapping, the government has to disprove wiretapping before it can bring the witness before a grand jury. On the basis of that case, charges against the others who refused to testify before the Harrisburg grand jury were dropped.

Terry was free.

The subsequent conspiracy trial of the Harrisburg Six, who became seven with the addition of the wife of one of the defendants, ended in a mistrial when the jury could not agree.

Surveillance ended. Terry went back to classes with a carefree spirit.

11. The Turning Point

> *To your endurance add godliness; to your godliness add brotherly affection; and to your brotherly affection add love.*
>
> Peter 1:7

The year 1971, her 22nd year, was a kind of watershed for Terry. Until now she had responded to needs as she saw them, intuitively and without hesitation, helping the disadvantaged—especially the children—in practical ways, and then moving on. Her instinctive reaction to the injustice of the fighting in Vietnam had involved her in the antiwar protests that were agitating the country and made her a part of the confrontation with the establishment.

Now it was time to put some structure into her life, and the future was problematic. Should she channel her energies into a standard career? Was a regular social service job her kind of thing? Could she work in a perfunctory institutional job? Or did the peace movement need her in a more concerted kind of commitment? There had been some estrangement with her family, and it needed healing. Then too, she wondered if she would settle into marriage. After the excitement and tension of the protest movement, it may now be time to turn to everyday concerns.

The sweet taste of victory came with a certificate in child care from Temple University. After tedious study, Terry became an authorized paraprofessional in social services. She applied for a job in the School of Social Administration, supervising students in their practicum. Her life settled into near normality. Even though she remained in contact with the peace people, she withdrew from close identity.

The war dragged on. Henry Kissinger announced on TV the night before the 1972 presidential election, "Peace is at hand." Nixon was re-elected and B52's continued to bomb Hanoi. Finally, a cease-fire in Vietnam, January 1973, ended the 18-year war. A peace group had formed in New Jersey, called the Camden 28. A number of familiar faces with a new organization asked Terry to be part of their defense committee. They had raided a draft board and were being tried. Terry rejected the offer. "She decided to take an establishment job," is the way D.A. put it.

Her priority was in the field of social service delivery, specifically child care. She hoped to work at St. Christopher's Hospital with students and young children. She was living on Apsley Street on the day of her interview and borrowed a skirt from D. A. to play the establishment role. She got the job.

Part of her work included teaching classes in the very course she had just completed. Her sister Joanne, who was eight years old, came to Terry's class on the day of a test. She took the test, just for fun, and got 98 out of 100 questions right. Joanne says she knew the answers because of caring for their retarded Uncle Harvey. Terry chided her for missing two.

In her work as a teacher, Terry watched the psychologist give intelligence tests to children. She thought of her lifelong conflict, believing her faculties were above average and, then, not being able to read or write without painful concentration. She read "morf" for "from," and "nosaer" for "reason." When she tried to write, the same jumble of letters stymied her. Then, she had to transpose the letters which took time and caused a great deal of anxiety. The psychologist gave her the WISC (Wechsler Intelligence Scale for Children) and the Stanford-Binet verbal intelligence test for adults. After diagnosing a combination of data from the tests, he was certain: Terry had dyslexia.

Her singular reaction was joyful relief. She was ebullient. She had identified the cause of frustration that had bedeviled her. It was a turning point in her life, a maturing.

Dyslexia is a learning disability that can be corrected if discovered in time. Terry was beyond the age to retrain the informational processes of her brain. A dyslexic person reads words from right to left. Words are heard in proper formation, but the letters reverse when written on paper or, worse yet, a typewriter. Dyslexic children are usually average in other skills. They develop above average social skills to compensate for the disability. They can manage in a regular classroom but rarely without special help in reading and writing.

As a child, Terry's home environment was a balance to her handicap. It was stimulating and active. The years in the family were, in fact, therapeutic. Without the antidotes, she could have become hopelessly inward and negative. The frustration caused by the disability affects children's personalities. They can become withdrawn, disagreeable. Terry channeled her frustrations into positive, constructive energy. She was influenced by her family's winning attitude toward life.

Even so, an inherent effect of learning disabilities is to be wary of lasting, one-to-one relationships, mainly because the affected person is insecure in accepting love. Marge McHugh believes Terry avoided being loved because of unselfishness. "Once you began to love her too much, she moved on." Terry moved in and out of people's lives. At times, she abruptly separated herself from close friends without explanation. On the other hand, the friendships formed at CSC and Search were deep, spiritual. She could resume a relationship after a long separation as if only a day had lapsed. It was the permanence of a loving commitment that she shunned. D. A. says Terry could not face accepting love from the Medical Mission Sisters and that was the main reason she did not become a full member of the community.

It is possible that accepting love from children, impoverished people, and the handicapped was safe. Nonetheless, love radiated from her.

Working at Temple brought Terry a steady income. Her dream of owning a car became a tangible reality. She bought a new, eight-passenger beige van. She also decided to look for an apartment. A member of Temple's faculty owned Mizpah Farm on the outskirts of the city, in Conshohocken. Terry rented an apartment over the barn.

A co-worker in Terry's department at school, Irene Holt, had been mulling over a way to care for children on weekends. The concept was new in Philadelphia. She consulted with the director of the Handicapped Children's Unit at St. Christopher's Hospital, Dr. John Bartram. There were no models, no precedents to follow and therefore no administrative snags. It would enrich the placement experience of students who were in the phase of the course that dealt with developmentally disabled children, including those with multiple handicaps. In lay terms, the mentally retarded and handicapped. Above all, it would help children and give parents a respite. The idea called for creative thinking, energy, and hard work. Terry was drawn to it like a moth to a flame.

The hospital owned a two-story rowhouse on Huntingdon Street near the main building. Two certified child-care workers and an aide/intern (a student) cared for four special guests on weekends.

Before the first guests came on a Friday afternoon in 1973, the program director and her staff burrowed through a mound of administrative details. The U.S. Department of Health, Education, and Welfare would not approve 412 W. Huntingdon Street as a health-care facility until it was renovated and met specifications.

Not quite as dingy as The Shoppe, the house needed cleaning and painting. Moreover, the hospital obtained the adjoining house and knocked out a wall, making 412 and 414 one residence. Terry acted quickly. Someone donated paint. A cadre of painters went to work. People from CSC, John Nevins, and Bud McHugh used rollers and brushes on ceilings and walls, window-sills, and door-jambs. Marge McHugh and Ronnie sewed draperies. Terry organized a work force; she supervised the project, doing much of the work herself. She built a wooden ramp so that children could easily walk from the back door to the yard. A small, cement fenced-in yard provided outdoor play space. The place passed HEW inspection.

Four young clients were brought to Respite Center by their parents and were left in Terry's care from three o'clock Friday until the same time Sunday. Ronnie helped when the program began.

Respite Center was a rallying point for Terry's family and a few friends. They came together to prepare a place of enjoyment for people in need. Terry's gift, her talent, was to respond in a rough and ready way to a specific need, creatively, and, in responding, to enlist the help of willing workers. She was often aware of needs before anyone else and had the vision to see solutions. The needs she met at The Shoppe influenced a neighborhood. Respite Center eventually reached out to parents who needed a break and to the children who needed to socialize with each other in a homey atmosphere.

The rehabilitation of the houses on Huntingdon Street and the service to the clients renewed Terry. It was like old times when John Nevins came to paint. She had come through the grueling experiences of the peace movement older and wiser. For a while she had been a celebrity, on TV newscasts, in the newspapers. She rode the crest of the wave as Vince DiPasquale had said. Gliding into the trough was difficult, although she had not crashed as he predicted. It had been hard for her to deal with herself as a person no longer in the spotlight. Later, working at Temple was another adjustment. She was thrust into an adult world. Nevins' friendship was constant even though Terry often brushed him off without a word of apology. She was cavalier in some personal relationships, especially with him. She could endure a project but did not want to persevere through the nitty-gritty of one-to-one, loving, relationships. Terry preferred to relate to people in a childlike way. Nevertheless, she was at ease with John Nevins. The frenzy of work at Respite Center rejuvenated family unity; the doldrums of recent years vanished.

Funding for Respite Center was never enough. Terry and all child-care workers donated their service on 30, or so, weekends throughout the year. Terry worked from early Friday, preparing, until late Sunday, closing. Then she returned to her regular job on Monday. She asked members of her softball team for money to pay for incidentals. The team agreed to play a benefit game in August, and it became an annual event.

The program director of Respite Center had not considered accepting adult clients until Terry mentioned it. Living with her Uncle Harvey, Terry realized the restrictions a special person places on a family, regardless of age. She persuaded the staff to receive adult guests along with children.

"Terry really got involved with the clients, especially the adults," a co-worker says. "She sang with them and got them to dance."

On summer afternoons, Terry took the guests in the van to her family's house. Marge, Joanne, and Helene picnicked with them on the lawn. Terry threw a frisbee. They fumbled it, always missing. She clapped as if they were experts.

Respite Center fared better than The Shoppe, which closed in the winter of 1970. Without heat and financial support, the building deteriorated. The Respite Center was a professional facility, an outreach of institutions: the hospital, the university, and Family Resource Service. Yet, it had the same spontaneity and affection. It was a home in the community, an extended family.

12. Once You Have Loved

By this we know that we abide in him and he in us, because he has given us of his own Spirit.

1 John 4:13

Part ownership of a horse named April was included in the apartment rental on Mizpah Farm. Terry was riding him in the paddock on a warm September evening when a car parked near the barn. A young man walked toward the fence, John Devenney. Terry dismounted, surprised and happy to see him. April munched on weeds as they talked.

"I'm glad I didn't try to find this place in the dark," John said.

Terry smiled, looked at him intently. "I'm glad you're here."

"Is that your horse?" he asked.

"Yeah, mine and three other people, I found out we've all been feeding him. I wondered why he got so fat."

"I've been wanting to talk with you, Terry. I miss you," he said.

"I guess I know how you feel." They walked April to his stall. "I've missed you too. Come on inside."

They sat on the sofa, drank beer, and reminisced. They laughed about Search weekends and the unforgettable atmosphere of Camp Neumann, caught up on news of friends. Terry sat quietly for a while.

"You know, since we parted," she said slowly, hesitating, "there hasn't been anyone that important, like the way you were."

"I wanted to know. It's the same with me," John said.

Terry leaned forward, ground out a cigarette butt in the ash tray. "And yet, I know I'm not ready for the kind of relationship we could have."

"A lot of people these days don't trust anything that smacks of permanence," John said, "not anything. Every time I start to believe in something, it's gone. We're trapped in the times we're living in."

After that evening, they saw each other often. Terry had few friends her age, most were older. They liked the simplicity of being together, wasting time on unimportant things. In those moments they were no longer John-leader, Terry-leader; they were two anonymous, carefree persons. John knew that Terry appeared to have it all together but was really in need of encouragement and love.

Their interest in Search picked up again. Camp Neumann was a world of its own; Terry found respite there. The people who were formed in the early days of CSC around Fathers Schmidt and Nevins became a leavening influence as young adults in Search. They were believable.

Terry noticed the span of years. Searchers seemed younger. At the same time, a subtle frustration oppressed her. She had outgrown Search socially even though her spiritual self longed for community. She found a supportive community in Search while she was in school. Being in touch again refreshed the precious, timeless bonds. When she looked for the whole community experience in one person, alone, it was like trying to put the ocean in a bottle. Her inner conflicts compounded.

Interestingly, in the years that followed CSC's first Operation Santa Claus, the program became a production. Terry stayed with it. The number of participants swelled to five, later, 800 students. A church basement, St. James in west Philadelphia, was a distribution center plus two more sites in outlying areas.

While Terry continued with Operation Santa Claus, she saw changes that disappointed her high hopes. Terry and Bob Todd had organized on the run. They could identify with a problem, move in, and act. Terry's advice, "hang loose," was her style. Spontaneity was braced with humor. The only time Bob McCarty saw her depressed was when a group of staffers sat around talking about the climate of CSC. Dilletantes bothered Terry. "Some people you don't see all year show up on Christmas Eve." Serving other people was an integral part of the lives of those in the group. They saw CSC moving away from poverty issues, away from risk taking. Sociologically, it changed focus. They preferred to have CSC resources serve the greatest need as they saw it: inner-city poor. Thereby the social conscience of students would be raised.

From the organizational point of view, CSC expanded to meet suburban needs—tutoring, visits to the elderly, services that are faithful to the gospel and would have gone unmet if all energy was funneled into the inner city. Equally important, the work is meant to develop the teenage high-school students who serve. Not everyone can be expected to be ready to deal with complicated, though urgent, social problems.

CSC and its counterpart, Search, have developed mature Christians who, indeed, are the hidden face of the church. They are signs of contradiction to the prevailing culture. Their social conscience was formed in a counter-cultural experience. Finding a new culture within a group that held the same new values, they were willing to act on those values.

Terry and Marisa Guerin were co-workers in the CYO and Search programs. Their background and perspective of youth ministry were similar. After college, Marisa followed her inclination for working within a structured environment, while Terry had the charism to relate to people personally. Now the representative for youth activities for the U.S. Catholic Conference, Marisa feels that youth ministry begins to fail when young people do not experience good parish life. "They have an idea of what it can be like from experiences outside the parish," she says. The so-called Christian community of a parish does not come near the reality of a community of Christians who are signs of contradiction. Instead, the parish often absorbs the prevailing secular culture. When that happens parishioners' energy and time go into activities that identify with church in name only. Reflection on ministries and spiritual growth is shunned. Fortunately, communities are rising in parishes whose life centers on worship and service. The community absorbs gospel values and without strain or embarrassment reflects on them and witnesses to the secular culture. The social conscience of youth in a parish cannot be developed if adults are not already aware that the gospel is a sign of contradiction.

"The attitude of young people depends on the attitude of people around them," Marisa says. "You can't teach new values to young people if they are not supported by adult leaders."

Terry herself continued to be a sign of contradiction, although it would not have occurred to her to see herself that way. She made no pretense of perfection. Personal conflicts were developing within; she thought she knew herself, but unresolved situations caused doubts; friendships that had been priorities were strung out; she seemed happiest at the height of action. The prophet Isaiah's poem of hope speaks to Terry:

> Even those who are young grow weak; . . .
> they will rise on wings like eagles;
> they will run and not get weary. . . . (Isaiah 40:30–31)

Her good sense of authenticity made her struggle for integrity. Her desire to serve people was solidly based on the gospel. However, the Word becomes a sterile rationale when it is read, even if taken seriously, in isolation, suspended from a supportive spiritual community.

Social service is one thing; social justice, another. Putting Matthew 25:31–46 into practice can be done by individuals or social service agencies for noble, human reasons: ". . . For I was hungry and you gave me food . . . I was a stranger and you welcomed me. . . ." Motivation is the key. Terry was motivated by the gospel imperative in all of her service to people. The relationships and projects in her life came together around the Eucharist in various liturgies. The Shoppe officially opened with Mass in what had been the dining room. Volunteers and neighborhood children gathered around Father Finley who made the place holy ground with the presence of the Lord.

While social service is both lofty and scientific, gospel values applied to the same service add a new dimension. There are inherent qualities of growth and healing. Social justice based on the gospels carries service to a higher level: It calls for insight, confrontation, and risk that science has not yet hypothesized. It is empty without faith and crass without love. It self-destructs without renewal at its source: a eucharistic community; personal and communal reflection.

Work around The Shoppe was centered in Christian social justice. It evolved from a group of people who came together over an unjust housing incident, who wanted racial harmony, and who tried to empower the powerless with a sense of their own worth. Terry was motivated to do things, sometimes grubby, sometimes heroic, by the spirit of Christ. She went ahead in spite of doubt but never seriously reflected on her own identity. Her vitality sparked life in others, nonetheless, and she operated from a support base of peers and adults who wanted to flesh-out the gospel.

The work at Respite Center was social service. It evolved from a group of people who had a humane desire to improve the lot of others and provide a unique education for child-care students. Respite Center's reason for existing had nothing to do with social justice, except for abiding by what is fair and equitable. Terry's motivation took her a sphere beyond human services. However she functioned outside of a supportive spiritual community. Therefore, communal, shared reflection flowing from the Word and Eucharist was missing in her work. If she had not known CSC or Search, had not been made vulnerable by love in a community experience, she would not have been confused by the lack of it. You can't miss what you don't know.

Terry's life was hyperactive. The kernel of confusion over community, or the lack of it, was of little concern at 23 or 24 years of age. She lived in the present; her future plans stretched only as far as summer trips. A young man, Mark, was enamored with Terry, "flipped over her." They went out together, socially. Mark wanted to see Terry on specific nights each week. She told him that schedules tied her down. They broke off. "Just because you show a little affection, they think you belong to them," she said.

The temper of the times was not conducive to a laid-back lifestyle. Young adults were still in the "me generation" in the early '70s which was quite likely a backlash from the war. Turmoil in the government accelerated. The Watergate burglary led to a full-blown Senate investigation, revealing that Nixon had full knowledge of the fiasco and had approved a cover-up. While the House Judiciary Committee was considering impeachment, the president resigned. Gerald Ford took office for a year and a half before Jimmy Carter was sworn in. National events, no longer remote, heightened anxiety. Permanence was a quality of another era.

Terry entered into the weekend programs at Respite Center with her typical zeal. Before special guests arrived on Friday, she visited their homes to obtain first-hand information concerning special needs, dietary and medical problems. The center was well supplied with toys for fun and learning. Terry prepared the meals, and guests and workers ate together. Her sister Maggie came to help occasionally. Respite Center was a community home away from home. The care lavished on the visitors made them sorry to leave on Sunday.

Clients come from various parts of the city into a section teaming with traffic. The residence directly faces Fairhill Square. Years ago, the square was a relief of green grass in the midst of narrow streets crowded with repetitive flat-front rowhouses. At the turn of the century, that part of Kensington thrived with German immigrants' families. Today, it is a densely populated mixture of white, black, and Hispanic people who project a profile of poverty.

The view from the small yard of Respite Center is no different from the clutter in the yards of Strawberry Mansion. The grass in Fairhill Square is trodden. Dry yellow dust swirls in the wind. To the left is the hospital. Respite Center is conveniently close by. It serves as a day-care center during the week. No one in the neighborhood questions its purpose. Yet, if a community home tried to occupy a house in a less rundown, more affluent section of the city, no doubt it would be quickly and forcefully opposed by neighbors. Enter, social justice.

When the center first began, Terry supervised every weekend. On Saturdays everyone in the house rode in her van to the zoo, or the circus, public gardens, the Flower Show or the ballet at the Academy of Music. Terry's softball team's benefit game provided funds for trips and entertainment expenses.

Clients stayed at Respite Center one or two weekends a year, making it available for others. Of course, there was a waiting list. Walter visited on an adult weekend. Although he was 25 years old, his mental development was no further than a three-year-old child. Physically, he was normal and so were his sex drives. Walter could neither be persuaded nor ordered to keep away from the aides. He listened only to Terry. At night, the girls on the staff slept with their beds jammed against the bedroom door.

Terry gave special care to a 35-year-old man who could do nothing for himself. She washed and fed him, changed his diapers.

A part of the work that annoyed Terry was the garbled speech of her weekend guests. She could not understand them. On an evening when she visited the Medical Mission Sisters on Pine Road, some of them were out but returned while she was there. When they came in she sensed something different about them. They seemed to "glow." She asked them where they had been. "You look different," she said. The sisters had been to a Charismatic prayer meeting. "You can pray in tongues, I can tell by looking at you," Terry told them.

The sensitivity to know when other people had the gift of tongues without hearing them was a new awareness for Terry. Still the guttural jumble of words from Respite Center clients irritated her. In exasperation, she prayed, "God, what good is it for me to know when people can pray in tongues when I can't tell what the clients who come to Respite Center are saying?" From then on, whether or not anyone could pray in tongues was not for her to know. Instead, she received a gift. "Right away," she told her sister Carol, "I understood every word the guests were saying. And I have ever since."

When the center developed a retinue of workers, Terry gave time to other people and interests. She was a valued peer counselor. Time and distance were not important if someone wanted to talk. She resisted schedules, partly because she wanted the freedom to respond to friends who needed a listener. Her friendship with John Devenney was not dependent on a weekly regimen of prescribed times for meeting. They loved each other and nothing had cooled the bond. Both knew it was time for a decision. Could they continue their relationship as close buddies or should they plan to marry? Terry had the use of the Medical Mission Sisters' cabin in the pines of Medford Lakes.

She suggested they go there, take some food for supper and talk about their future together.

John made a fire in the fireplace, opened a beer, and settled in a lounge chair to watch the Penn State game on TV. While Terry was preparing supper, she heard the blare of the TV, charged out of the kitchen and flicked off the switch. "Oh, no you don't," she said, "we're not married yet. I'm not playing the housewife role while you sit with your feet propped up watching the tube."

After supper they sat by the fireplace, sipping wine. They were both involved in the problems of other people's lives. The possibility of going to the Medical Missions was still in the back of Terry's mind. Whether she went or not, ministering to other people gave purpose to life more than a total commitment to one person in marriage. Being at the lake was a test for Terry. She would not say, bluntly, that she wanted to follow Christ. The inner direction that had guided her through the doubts of recent years, through inner-city tensions, through the surveillance and trial still burned within. She and John were buddies. Her commitment to him could go no further than that. It was not an easy decision. John hugged her while she cried.

13. Leaders Live a Lonely Life

For most who live hell is never know-
ing who they are. The Singer knew
and knowing was his torment.

Calvin Miller
The Singer

A year-long birthday party began on January 1, 1976:
cities and towns of America celebrated the Bicentennial.
Philadelphia made 1776 come alive. The Liberty Bell
reigned majestically in its glass house on Independence
Mall. From early in the morning until dark on New Year's
Day, the Mummers paraded north on Broad Street in fes-
tive costumes.

The Bicentennial theme carried through the annual
parish picnic on Memorial Day. Red, white, and blue paper
cloths covered tables. Small flags with the thirteen stars
decorated cakes. The McHugh contingent gathered
around the table Terry reserved.

At the end of the day, 7:30 p.m. to be precise, Terry
drove up Germantown Avenue on the way to her apartment. The avenue is narrow and winding with trolley
tracks in the center. She saw a car coming toward her,
moving into her lane. Another car passed her from behind
and nearly clipped the van. Terry swerved. The oncoming
car hit her head-on. She lay near the door of the van which
was damaged beyond repair. In pain, severely hurt, she

waited for the rescue squad. Her brother Hugh drove down the same street shortly after the crash. With a sickening feeling, he recognized the van. Terry cried when she saw him and asked him to stay with her. Hugh called their parents from the emergency room of the hospital. Terry's leg, arm, and two ribs were broken. One side of her body was bruised. When she was able to leave the hospital, she went home to recuperate. It was a long, tedious summer.

The semester had ended at Temple, and Respite Center functioned well without her. Terry could have enjoyed the vacation. She had looked forward to playing softball. The team was aiming for its fourth championship. She liked playing tennis with John Nevins. And, of first priority, she could spend time with friends who relied on her. The Eucharistic Congress was due in Philadelphia but she shied away from the snail's pace of organizing mammoth events. It held no appeal.

Her plans were thwarted, and it frustrated her. The van was demolished; it depressed her. An unbearable restlessness overcame her as she lay on the sofa, staring at the ceiling. Thrust back into the family house after living alone aggravated her difficulties. Marge related to her as parent to child, the bent of mothers, not as mother to young adult.

The tent. She remembered the tent they used for camping. Charles set it up on the lawn, strung an extension cord to a lamp and TV, unrolled her sleeping bag. Terry camped out and her New Testament went with her. She healed quickly but not cheerfully. The family noticed that she was in a funk.

As soon as her casts were removed, Charlie took her to look for another van. They avoided the showroom of the automobile dealer and went to the used-car lot. She paid cash for her new-used van rather than go in debt. Her mood improved: she was mobile.

In August, friends in the Department of Youth Activities who were working on the Eucharistic Congress persuaded her to help. CSC-CYO added many alphabet programs and administered them through the department (DYA). Father Schmidt was named Monsignor. Once again, a van served Terry's willingness to accommodate requests for help. Her attitude toward the Congress, however, was one of reserve, bordering on disdain. Terry's understanding of Eucharist was experiential communal sharing. She entered into the joy and sorrow of other people's lives through the real, though intangible, bond that comes from and goes back to the table of the Lord.

True, it was a reality to be celebrated by all people in a joyous meeting such as the Congress. In Terry's experience of church, nonetheless, the institution had assumed a powerful, remote stance that seemed to make the essence of Eucharist subordinate.

She did not construct or verbalize a theology of Eucharist. She lived it. Her presence to other people was an undistracted, undiminished flow from its source, the presence of the Lord through Eucharist and grace. While listening to someone, Terry was not consciously aware of her gift of presence. She cared deeply about people and expressed it in attentiveness.

"She hated a showy kind of thing that didn't have a solid base in service," John Nevins says. She judged the Eucharistic Congress would be more talk than action where it was needed. "When situations are not as good as they could be, when you're sensitive to the good way things could be and they're not, it hurts," she told Nevins. Her impression changed when she heard Dom Helder Camara, archbishop of Recife, Brazil, challenge complacency toward the poor.

While the Congress was meeting, a young friend from CSC, Eileen Potts, was seriously ill in the hospital. She wanted to meet Mother Theresa who had come from Calcutta, India. Terry was asked to drive Mother Theresa to visit Eileen. The closeness of escorting the demure nun overwhelmed Terry. She was swept into a change of heart by the simplicity of the person who owned only two saris, one to wear while the other was laundered; who gave her energy to rescuing abandoned infants and gave dignity to dying people. Terry's vitality was restored.

A room in the basement of McHugh's house was "Terry's Den." She lived in it and gave up her apartment. It offered some solitude. She was becoming more reflective, conscious of her own mortality. American society preserves childhood and adolescence. It romanticizes the teenage years, encouraging a long postponement of decisions about future goals. Not only was Terry caught in that, her teenage years went quickly in the hype of dedication to the poor and peace. With it all, she enjoyed life. To leave a fun situation and go to help someone was no sacrifice. When others might do the same service, bear with it and mark time, it was an integral part of Terry's life.

"She was an average kid," Joe Corley says, "she liked parties and drank beer, but when Christian values were threatened she went after it like a shark."

Her response to threatened Christian values caused her to set aside some of the average growth in that time of her life. There had been no space or time to questions who she really was or where her future was going. At age 26 the symbols and activities with which she had identified earlier were gone. Terry found her identity in situations and environments that needed her talents. When the situation was gone or she left the environment, her perspective of herself, her identity, was also gone.

While Terry reflected on projects and her part in them, she rarely looked into herself. Friends were surprised to hear her talk about her personal life. Even then, she felt free to talk only with people who had been constants in the past ten years. Terry had many friends, but the depth of the friendships varied, and only the constants were privy to her self-reflection.

After a set of tennis, John Nevins and Terry talked through lunch. He goaded her to think about long-term goals. She said, "I knew it. I knew you were going to bring that up. I just knew it! Later. I'll talk about it later." She wanted to say "yes" to everything in her life. Consequently she did not make a firm commitment to one goal or one relationship. She was ambivalent about John Nevins, too. She wanted his friendship and had related well as teenager/priest. It was awkward to relate as young woman/priest. She was his near-peer.

When she left him to return home, he said, "Give a call." Although she said she would, the odds were against her calling him. Some people credit her for detachment, and there is no doubt she did not cling to this world's goods nor to any special person. However, to neglect to call was more of a quirk than a virtue. She neglected to keep in touch in the way people who loved her would have liked.

On the other hand, her friends knew that they could call her anytime, day or night, if they needed her. She helped more people move than Joe Corley can count. He remembers, "I was stuck with bills for U-Haul rentals."

Beth McMullen was a constant for Terry. After high school their lives went in different directions but their friendship survived. Beth knew how deeply Terry cared about people. Even though she appeared unflappable, Beth churned inwardly. When her father died, Terry comforted her. Terry knew she had a hard time expressing feelings about her personal life and suggested they have a code. If Beth wanted to talk, regardless of the hour, she was to call Terry and say, "I'm letting you know." Terry promised to come immediately. If Terry was not at home, Beth was to leave the coded message with Marge McHugh, "Tell Terry I'm letting her know," and Marge knew what it meant. "No matter where you are or what time it is, I'll come," Terry said. Beth drew strength from the promise.

She drove Terry home one evening after a movie. A Barbra Streisand song came on the car radio as they neared McHugh's house. Terry asked her to drive around the block, she wanted to hear the song. She put her head back and went to sleep. When she woke she grabbed Beth's hand. Beth thought Terry felt lonely, sad. "She had no one person to relate to, no permanent relationship."

Friends visited Terry in her den. Not everyone agreed with Terry's views and weighty discussions flared occasionally. Beth McMullen wrote about it:

> Bunny and Terry were having a fight
> As usual, just the other night.
> Terry argues rights for the blacks,
> While Bunny sits, making cracks.

They're poor and oppressed not by choice.
"Don't blame me!" Bunny voiced.

Bunny works and saves her money,
While the blacks sit home like bees making honey.
Thinking of them on welfare lists
Makes Bunny clench her fists.
Terry says they're entitled to funds.
Bunny says, "Not from me working off my buns!"

Then when they talk of prison reform
I can feel in my bones the start of a storm.
Terry believes in making cons better,
Don't follow the law to the letter.
Staying in cells is not the way
To learn to live in society someday.

"Go ahead," says Bunny, "spend my bread,
tax me and tax me until I am dead.
It won't do one bit of good
To try to reform a hood.
They're out on parole for barely a day
Before they are looking for someone to slay.

Bunny believes she has the proof,
An eye for an eye, a tooth for a tooth.
Terry's committed to helping the weak,
Follow the Lord, turn the other cheek.
They argue in circles, getting nowhere.
Until they're ready to tear their hair.
I have to admit each has a theory,
But, O God, it makes me weary.

Terry was striving to be good in a world that was not
good, trying to be holy but not churchy. She winced at the
word "holy" being applied to her. She preferred to be

recognized as a decent person who did what she knew in her heart she had to do. She took her gifts and used them to the fullest: the effort combined with goodness is holiness.

She was becoming aware of her limitations. It had never occurred to her that she might fail at anything. The years of struggling through dyslexia toughened her approach to life. Now, in the time of reflection, she was beginning to face the concept of failure. Only good people are concerned about being good. In spite of her close family and many friends, Terry had a tendency to belittle herself, not only in self-effacement but in low self-esteem. She was afraid to accept love.

When a person has one skill, or one affinity, deciding on a goal is simple. However, when a person has a variety of skills, a wealth of gifts, the options compound. In that event, to say "yes" to one option and focus energy on the choice involves risk and faith. Terry knew that she had the skills and talents to go in many directions. "She wanted to mother the whole world," John McNamee says. "She had such a deep involvement, she could not fit into any one category." Her options caused a crisis of decision that got her down. Her gifts were a burden.

In a Peanuts cartoon, Charles Schulz shows Linus coming home from school with a B+ on his report card. His parents boo. Linus says, "There's no heavier burden than a great potential."

In warm weather Terry wore cut-offs over a tank suit. When the tank suit wore thin, she patched it. She accommodated custom and dressed accordingly when the occasion called for it, looking self-possessed in a plaid skirt, turtleneck sweater, and beige jacket. A Grecian-style white dress was on hand for more formal gatherings. She had a collection of lapel buttons for every cause that came down the pike.

Her personal possessions satisfied basic needs. Beyond her simplicity in appearance, there was a storehouse of versatility and resourcefulness. She responded instantly to problems. She was in a bar in Roxborough one evening with Kenny Houston. Three angry young men burst in looking for someone. Pistols in hand, they shot at random. Patrons scrambled under tables, all but Terry. She stood and faced them then walked toward them. As she talked, they put the guns away and left. On the way out the door one turned to her and said, "See ya around." She said, "Yeah, see you in jail."

When Brother Joseph Schmidt first met Terry her personality impressed him. He was the first director of the Discovery Leadership Institute in 1971. DLI is a year-round program that develops leadership in teenagers, the majority of whom are black boys. They give twelve hours of service a week and build a strong community within the program. Outward Bound is part of DLI training. Terry worked with Brother Joe on camping trips and retreat weekends.

He was a constant for Terry. Although she came in and out of his life, he saw her need for a long-term friendship. He knew her depth and saw her become reflective. He noticed that she had not theorized over serving people. If a situation or person clicked, she went into action. She went on her intuitions. He believes she waited too long to reflect on how her involvements affected her life. All the while, she was her own person and, at last, getting in touch with herself. "That is the process of holiness, getting in touch with yourself," he says.

Brother Joe compares Terry to St. Therese of Lesieux,

the Little Flower, an unlikely parallel considering the contrast in demeanor and lifestyles. His comparison searches beneath the surface to their motivation and endurance.

"St. Therese accepted the things in her environment that were right for the way she was meant to be," Brother Joe says. "In screening out things that are not essential you ruffle feathers because you eliminate meaningless rules and regulations. They are the very things institutions are trying to maintain.

"The person who tries to live authentically finds conflict. In the struggle, holiness develops because in every step of the way the person has to be true to himself or herself. More than that, the person has to be honest and faithful to the commitment to other *people*."

She had no guilt feelings about not being pious according to the definition of prescribed pious devotions. Terry neither wanted to nor could define the abstractions of her spiritual life. She fleshed them out, knowing that prayer and persons are authentic when they are rooted in reality.

"Terry's spirituality was rooted in her," Brother Joe says. "She shunned piosity and religious expressions that were not authentic to her personally and that alone is significant. She had a sense of personal honesty which I found profound."

Some friends compare Terry with Thomas Merton, the Trappist monk and poet, another incongruous pairing. Both thought all violence was wrong and spoke against the Vietnam war; both had a vision of where the black community was going years before others became aware. Merton once lived in the black ghetto in Harlem. Jeanne Walsh respects Terry's intense spirituality. "There was a call inside her that kept her going." A friend of Jeanne's who knew Merton said, "He drank beer with the rest of us when he came into town from the abbey and his laugh was the loudest." Both Terry and Merton had no wish to be different from everyone else.

Marisa Geurin is convinced that Terry's ability to be present, to listen and empower people was a charism. Her ministry to youth was an example of a journey in faith. Marisa believes Terry's faith was her greatest gift. "Most adults haven't searched for or owned their faith but simply belong to a church all their lives and don't think twice about it."

Working in Temple's child-care program became uncomfortably political. Terry was caught in conflicts between mutual friends. A person she had trusted let her down. Worse yet, political favoritism chafed at her sense of honesty. While she was supervising a group of students, she recommended flunking one in particular. A person higher up in the administration made certain the student passed. Terry was disillusioned. In the winter of 1977 she was distressed by the wrangling and she quit. Her one link with a permanent involvement was gone. The trauma was shattering. Her life fragmented and she grasped for meaning. Days were aimless.

She applied for unemployment compensation and received it. She shared a portion of the compensation with a divorced parent of four children, a young woman in the neighborhood. Then Terry took a part-time job in a flower shop.

Purpose in life eluded her. She had been the leader, the visionary. People who resisted leaving a secure niche had followed Terry, finding safety in her confidence and humor. She had outgrown the commitments that would have served as a refuge from hurt. There was no supportive spiritual community to provide balm for her spirit.

She applied to the Brotherhood of Carpenters for an apprenticeship as a millwright—the work her father had done for 25 years. The union refused her because she was female. However, her father says she could have done the job better than some men.

A friend, another Theresa, was in the Merchant Marine. After hearing about her work and travels, Terry considered going to sea. She applied for a job on an Atlantic Refining Company tanker. The Coast Guard cleared her papers and she waited for Merchant Marine approval.

The sailing date was in September.

14. Outward Bound

> *It is our willingness to die for our ideals that makes it possible for those ideals to live.*
>
> *Robert F. Kennedy*
> A New Day

Terry's aimless days in the spring were soon filled. She became a listener and advocate for people in the neighborhood. At least ten families found a bit of relief through her empathy. Her life was fragmented, nonetheless. She gave her attention to other people while she was "treading water," as John Nevins puts it. "She was floating."

Marge McHugh says life with her at that time was hectic. Terry was distant. She went out of the house with no word of when she would return. Some nights she did not return and stayed away for days. A neighborhood bar was the favorite meeting place for Terry and her local friends. Marge was upset; she saw her daughter wasting her life.

Marge confronted Terry, calling her into Maggie's room on a Sunday afternoon. "Terry, I have got to talk with you. What are you doing with your time? Where are you going? You stay away. You don't call. I love you and I worry about you."

It was an emotional two hours.

Terry told her mother, "You don't understand my

friends. They have problems and I'm trying to help them. You're too critical of me and them. That's why I don't bring them here. That's why I stay away."

Marge insisted that she did not want Terry to be misled by other people she knew who were drinking heavily and smoking dope.

"Why didn't you tell me if you thought I was doing things you worry about? Why didn't you tell me to 'knock it off?" Terry asked. "I love you and Dad. I know you were critical because you want to help me."

Their reconciliation was a dramatic moment that affected both lives. Marge's trust in Terry was restored. Terry found the security she needed while she floundered through uncertainties. From then on, she was lighthearted and cheerful in the house and invited friends to visit again.

Kenny Houston came for lunch one day. He was working for the Discovery Leadership Institute at the time. Kenny was a constant for Terry. The friendship that began in a Search football scrimmage deepened over the years. Her unique humor appealed to him. "She was extremely versatile and resourceful," Kenny says. "She came up with instant solutions to problems." Kenny went to college after serving in the army. He stayed in touch with Terry, always maintaining a working relationship with youth ministries.

Kenny needed someone to supervise five teenage boys on Outward Bound in Maine in July, and he asked Terry to consider going. She knew about Outward Bound from Brother Joe Schmidt. He and Kenny had been the first to go from DLI. Terry didn't hesitate. She agreed to follow the training schedule in order to be in condition for survival camping. It required a physical exam, fifty push-ups and two miles of jogging each day for a month, a canoe trip and caving. Kenny arranged the caving expedition and canoe trip.

Terry's spirit quickened. She felt the at-homeness of being involved in a DLI activity. The purpose in taking the boys to Maine was in harmony with what had motivated her in the happy times of the Community Service Corps, Search, and the unforgettable years around Strawberry Mansion. Kenny's request was a reprieve from the emptiness of life.

She told John Nevins about Outward Bound. He was pleased that she had a chance to get away. Perhaps she could get in touch with the direction her life should take. When they were together for tennis or golf, he could see that she was preoccupied with thoughts she could not express.

She called him early in June and asked him to go with her to a Liv Ullman play in New York City. She knew he could get tickets through a friend. Her van was in the repair shop and she asked him to drive. He offered her his car. He was busy clearing up school business and could not spare the time. A matinee in New York would take all of Wednesday out of his week. Terry pressed him. There was an insistence in her voice. Giving in, he went reluctantly.

While riding on the New Jersey turnpike, Terry reminisced. An innate part of her personality was silence about herself. She also maintained a separateness in varying phases and groups in her life: Search friends did not know about Respite Center; the softball team thought the games were her primary, consuming interest. Under the hype of activity, Terry could, at times, be a withdrawn, quiet person. John Nevins had tried many times to give her a chance to talk about herself, and she closed him off decisively. On the way to New York, she released a spate of memories and impressions that had been sealed within her. He watched her as she spoke in a soliloquy. She laughed as she recalled Search weekends. He could sense a faint melancholy.

They went to the Imperial Theatre to see "Agatha Christie." During the intermission Terry bought him a drink. Again, she rehashed events in her life that had special meaning. He realized she needed him to listen.

When the matinee was over they had an early dinner and walked down Broadway to the Avenue of the Americas. A friend had an art exhibit somewhere in the area. By the time they reached 38th Street, they knew the exhibit would be closed, so they returned to Broadway. Terry, the impish nonconformist, took a step ahead of John. She said, "I'll race you," and took off. Her flip-flops clopped as her feet hit the pavement. John jogged after her at no easy pace, Terry was in condition for Outward Bound. The inane scene, man-chasing-girl up Broadway, was a normal occurrence from her outlook, a fun thing to do. Terry glanced back at him and laughed.

Duffy Square and the lights of the newscasts on the old Times building came into view. When she approached 42nd Street, she stopped abruptly, turned and reached out for him. Putting her hands on his shoulders, she lowered her head and cried. While they stood there, she sobbed. Passersby glanced disinterestedly, then continued on. He motioned toward the curb. They crouched down and sat amid the roar of traffic. He waited for her to stop crying. She told him of her frustrations and disillusions.

"Look at these people. If somebody got hit here, nobody would bother to help!"

She cried again. Turning to John, she was quiet, hesitated for a moment and said slowly, "I trust you."

Then she waited as if to gain courage, "Will you help me?"

She put her arm around him and they walked slowly up Broadway, stopping once or twice while she talked freely about herself.

"What keeps you going?" she asked.

"Well, you know, I have friends and then there's prayer," he answered.

"You mean Jesus," she said.

"Yes, I mean Jesus."

"Am I your friend?" She looked at him.

"You've always been my friend, you know. Yes, you're my friend," he said.

"Do you believe in me?" she asked, emphatically.

"Yes, I believe in you."

On the way back to Philadelphia Terry continued talking, trusting him, comfortable in his constancy.

If the root causes of Terry's emotional crisis could have been described, she might have dealt with them. She was struggling with her own identity and feeling insecure. It meant a lot to know that people believed in her. She knew they believed in projects, but when it came time to separate persons from projects she was not sure anyone believed in her as a person. Some people had said they loved her, and she had not responded to their love. All of a sudden, in the noise of Broadway, she knew the importance of being loved.

In the middle of June, Skip Gaus asked Kenny Houston and Terry to go caving in West Virginia. Skip took a group of boys from De La Salle Vocational school on "Project Alive." Caving was part of the requirement of conditioning for Outward Bound.

They double-checked their equipment at the entrance to Hell Hole cave, one of the largest caves in the country. Terry, like the others, wore coveralls, a long-sleeve shirt, gloves, and a yellow hard hat. She fastened a seat of webbing around her and prepared to descend.

Hell Hole Cave is 187 feet into the earth. As cavers descend on a thin nylon rope, the cave expands like the dome of a cathedral. Looking up, the cave is shaped like a spire, pointing to a small opening of light. The drop is not straight down but angular and jagged. A unique breed of bats swoop toward the floor of the cave. When everyone in the group reached the bottom they lingered a while before ascending. Twenty boys ascended before Terry, leaving four at the base.

Terry prepared to ascend and secured her shoulder harness to the nylon rope. The harness attached to an "ascender" on her feet. She slid one foot up the rope. It clamped in place while she drew the other foot up. While one foot is being drawn up, the knee of the secure leg is bent in a kneeling position. Halfway up the rope, in a dark chamber nine stories high, Terry's left foot was clamped in position but her right foot slipped out of the "ascender." She lost her grip and dangled. Her left foot and knee were hooked to the rope while she swung around. She panicked. Screamed. Out of control. There was nothing to grab. No one was there to push her body into a position to resume ascending.

The boys who were outside tied a rope to the nylon rope, pulled, hauled, and finally hoisted Terry to a jutting ledge of rock. Groping in the darkness, she reassembled the clamps and harness. She climbed to daylight. Standing on firm ground under the open sky, she gained composure.

It was the first time Kenny and Skip had seen Terry out of control. They had never seen her scared, much less, panic. In that horrifying situation, other people had to make decisions for her. Once again, she experienced surrender and reached for help from people who loved her.

Shortly after returning from West Virginia, Kenny planned the canoe trip. He and Terry went to the Mullica river in South Jersey. They rented a canoe and were transported several miles upstream. The river can provide a leisurely, scenic glide through the Pine Barrens. As it swirls in a dense tract of wilderness the sky overhead is laced with leafy branches of trees. At times the dark cedar water is narrow and deep, then widens and flows past sunny stretches of sandy beach.

"How long is this trip?" Terry asked Kenny.

"Oh, it takes about five hours if the water's fast," he said.

"That long! I have to be back in Philly by six."

"We have portages on this river, girl. You want me to run with this barge?"

They rushed down the river and back to the city. Terry had to play in a softball game. She managed the team and wanted to succeed as the first female manager in the league.

She interrupted her preparations for Hurricane Island to plan a surprise birthday party for an aunt who was 80 years old. In recent weeks Terry had had a yearning for a reunion of her own friends. She wanted to gather everyone she had known in the past ten years. She asked

John Nevins to think of an appropriate place to have a liturgy followed by a party.

The birthday party partially satisfied her desire. It was a family reunion, a special time of happiness and warmth. While her aunt was pleased, Terry's ever-present smile expressed her joy in doing something of value for someone else.

Epilogue

Terry arrived in Brigantine about ten o'clock Friday evening, July 1. She spent two hours with her family and said goodbye shortly after midnight. She drove to Ocean City, a nearby shore resort, to visit relatives. From there, she would return home and leave for Outward Bound.

Between Brigantine and Ocean City the rear tire blew. The van careened off an embankment, turned over, and caught fire. Terry was knocked unconscious and died in the burning van.

John Nevins called Joe Corley early Saturday morning and told him. When Joe said Mass that day the gospel was about the man who built bigger barns to store all his goods "and God said, this very night you will have to give up your life." Joe thought the words spoke of Terry because she had not held on to anything and was ready.

John Devenney was in the kitchen of Camp Neumann Saturday morning preparing breakfast for 200 campers. Bob McCarty came in and said, "One of the McHughs died in an accident." He left and returned in a short while. "It was Terry," he said. John finished what he was doing and went to his cabin, alone. He expressed his feelings in a poem:

> Far, fly away
> burning jewel of my growing days
> whose love first taught

this empty heart to sing
and dance with enthusiasm for life.

Far, fly away
sweet Terry,
to a more solitary, more free
life with Christ.

How strange,
that my sweet sister,
should join today,
her burnt and broken brothers.

by John Devenney 7/2/77

"If she ended the Vietnam war singlehanded," John Devenney said, "if she fed every black kid in Philly, she would
not have felt her life had been complete. The one thing
Terry needed was to come together with Christ and in her
dying she did just that."

The eulogy given at Robert Kennedy's funeral by his
brother Edward seems appropriate for Terry:

> She need not be idealized or enlarged in death beyond what
> she was in life. She should be remembered simply as a good
> and decent person who saw wrong and tried to right it, saw
> suffering and tried to heal it, saw war and tried to stop it.

> Those of us who loved her pray that what she was to us, and
> what she wished for others, will someday come to pass for all
> the world.

A few weeks later, Marge McHugh looked through Terry's belongings. In a drawer, she found the album, "Journey to Jesus," that Terry had often played. Marge placed it
on the stereo and listened, waiting for the last song, one
written by Barbara Sipple called "Take Me Home."

I been young and I been restless, I been slippery in the mind,
Been dreamin 'bout the places that nobody ever finds,
I been up and down and all around and I been there all alone,
But one of these roads is bound to take me home.

I been set up by some people who were not too nice to know,
Then I come to get the feeling that it's time for me to go,
And I say to myself you got to learn to make it on your own,
And one of these roads is bound to take me home.

Then I turned my eyes to Jesus and I found the road to prayer,
And everyday He takes me home and I find comfort there,
And my heart is not so heavy and my thoughts are not so blown,
And one of these roads has finally led me home.